ESSENCE

This Personal Journal Belongs To

_____

Welcome to a journey to freedom.

Discovering a Pathway to Our New Existence, Leading Us to 21st-Century Living

ESSENCE
**Expanding Self-Awareness,
Awakening Inspiration,
Unleashing Our Power From Within**

21stCenturyParadigm.com

REGENERATING HUMANITY
**Seeing, Trusting, and Taking
the eXpansive Path to
21st-Century Living**

RegeneratingHumanity.com

THE 21st-CENTURY ALCHEMIST
**A Journey in Unleashing
Our Hidden Powers**

The21stCenturyAlchemist.com

FIRST BOOK ~ EXPANSION

ESSENCE is about the expansion of self-awareness, seeing ourselves through a much more eXpansive perspective, awakening our inspiration, and unleashing our power from within. Inspired action is key to regenerating ourselves and the lives we are living.

SECOND BOOK ~ VISION

REGENERATING HUMANITY is about a vision of a pathway leading us to our new 21st-century existence of human-life on Mother Earth filled with love, joy, freedom, abundance, and peace. Establishing a new vision is key to regenerating humanity. Once we agree, perspectively align, deeply feel, and energetically vibrate this new vision, then so it becomes.

THIRD BOOK ~ CREATION

THE 21ST-CENTURY ALCHEMIST is an insightful parable about a teenage girl who is dissatisfied with her life, and decides to embark on a journey across the world with her two best friends, in search of how to create a meaningful life in the 21st century. On their journey, they meet a wise elder, named Kali, who teaches them that the answers they are seeking already reside within themselves, and through unleashing their hidden powers, they are able to create the life they desire.

Available on Amazon
in Print and eBook

Expanding Self-Awareness,
Awakening Inspiration,
Unleashing Our Power From Within

Mind ✿ Body ✿ Spirit ✿ Soul

Ann Emerson
Bo Lockwood

Princeton, New Jersey • princetongreen.org

"In *Essence*, Ann Emerson and Bo Lockwood's inspirational energy offers all of us an easy, step-by-step manual for living our life in the 21st century—with true freedom and joy, on our own terms. *Essence* offers practical advice on how to apply Spiritual principles to live authentically with more awareness and love versus scarcity and fear. It also brings importance to how we *are* Nature, and the way we care for the environment is a reflection of how we care for ourselves. *Essence* has a unique vibe that is like Hemingway's—written in a simple, direct, succinct style that powerfully engages a beginner as well as an advanced reader in this genre of reading."

Alyona Bauer, D.M.D., M.A.
Spiritual Psychologist
Coauthor, *Regenerating Humanity*

"In their well-organized treatise on the power of co-creation, Ann Emerson and Bo Lockwood present an ideology, that when taken to heart, will help realize the inception of a higher-conscious paradigm for ourselves and all of humankind. *Essence* packs a powerful message that involves the reader in an interactive manner, helping each person to reflect and digest the deeper meaning of the greatest transition they will ever experience."

Rev. Arlene Rose Curley, Ph.D.
Author, *Completing the Seven* and *The Eighth Gate*
Director, Greenshire Arts Consortium

For those of us who have challenges
with reading books all the way through,
simply hold this book over your third eye
(on your forehead, just above the eyebrows),
calm down by quieting your mind,
and ask yourself:

What do I need to see and learn about myself today?

Then let your fingers guide you to the
section of the book that speaks with you.

We are here, serving you by supporting
the awakening of your Soul.

As your Soul awakens,
your inspiration does, too.

If you are open to receiving free
inspirational ideas that support your awakening,
simply visit our Web site to register:

21stCenturyParadigm.com/Inspiration/

or send an email to:

Inspiration@21stCenturyParadigm.com

You will immediately receive an automated email
reply with the options to register.

Then you will begin receiving inspired energy
that awakens your Soul.

Published by Princeton Green Publishing, a division of Princeton Green LLC, 888.995.5630, princetongreen.org.

Copyright © 2017 Princeton Green LLC. All rights reserved.
First edition 2014. Second edition 2017.

Foreword: Dana B. Lichtstrahl
Editors: Elizabeth Ely, Mindy Knapp
Cover Design: Peter van Geldern
Earth Art: Jacob Lichtstrahl
PGP Hazel Art: Olivia Lockwood

Without limiting the rights under copyright reserved above, no part of this publication may be reproduced, stored in, or introduced into a retrieval system, or transmitted, in any form or by any means (electronic, mechanical, photocopying, recording or otherwise), without the prior written permission of both the copyright owner and the publisher of this book.

The scanning, uploading, and distribution of this book via the Internet or via any other means without the permission of the copyright owner and the publisher is illegal, and punishable by law. Please purchase only authorized electronic editions, and do not participate in or encourage electronic piracy of copyrightable materials. Your support of the authors' rights is appreciated.

ISBN-13: 978-0-9855838-0-4

Printing/manufacturing information for this book may be found on the last page.

DEDICATION

Ann Emerson

I dedicate this book to my five children—
Jack, Steve, Phil, Alicia, and Peter,
as well as their spouses,
Jody, Anne, Peg, and Joanie.
And to my 10 grandchildren—
Kate, Emily, Mara, Abby, Kendall, Sean, Pete,
Shannah, Ben, and Josh.
You are the fire in my heart that makes all of
my life meaningful.
I also dedicate this book to the children of the
Earth, as they're our future. May this book
expand their self-awareness and be a blessing
to all who read it.

Mom ~ Gram ~ Ann

Bo Lockwood

I dedicate this book to my daughters—
Olivia and Hannah; to my parents—Toni and Jim;
to my brothers—Dave and Mike; to my reflection—
Alyona; and to my extended family—Dale, Rhonda,
Megan, Matt, Brian, Sam, James, Braydon, James,
Lisa, Paul, Grace, Morgan, Hazel, Seth,
Dana, Jake, and Nikki. May this book help to fully
awaken your Souls, living life with more love, joy,
freedom, abundance, and peace. I love you.

Dad ~ Bo

CONTENTS

Foreword	xix
Preface	xxi
Introduction	1
Aspect #1 ~ Self-Awareness	10
Aspect #2 ~ Infinite Being	16
Aspect #3 ~ Connectedness	22
Aspect #4 ~ Balance	28
Aspect #5 ~ Regenerative Living	34
Aspect #6 ~ Learning	40
Aspect #7 ~ Wisdom	46
Aspect #8 ~ Purpose	52
Aspect #9 ~ Change	58
Aspect #10 ~ Heart-Centeredness	64
Aspect #11 ~ Forgiveness	70
Aspect #12 ~ Self-Love	76
Aspect #13 ~ God Within	82
Aspect #14 ~ Honesty	88

Aspect #15 ~ Authenticity	94
Aspect #16 ~ Truth	100
Aspect #17 ~ Trust	106
Aspect #18 ~ Hope	112
Aspect #19 ~ Faith	118
Aspect #20 ~ Belief	124
Aspect #21 ~ Divine Will	130
Aspect #22 ~ Patience	136
Aspect #23 ~ Bravery	142
Aspect #24 ~ Perseverance	148
Aspect #25 ~ Fortitude	154
Aspect #26 ~ Gratitude	160
Aspect #27 ~ Humility	166
Aspect #28 ~ Simplicity	172
Aspect #29 ~ Collaboration	178
Aspect #30 ~ Mind Energy	184
Aspect #31 ~ Body Energy	190
Aspect #32 ~ Spirit Energy	196
Aspect #33 ~ Present Time	202
Aspect #34 ~ Vision	208
Aspect #35 ~ Focus	214
Aspect #36 ~ Contemplation	220

Aspect #37 ~ Acceptance	226
Aspect #38 ~ Willingness	232
Aspect #39 ~ Money Energy	238
Aspect #40 ~ Compassion	244
Aspect #41 ~ Giving & Receiving	250
Aspect #42 ~ Equality	256
Aspect #43 ~ Unity	262
Aspect #44 ~ Love	268
Awakening	275
Decision Time	279
Personal Vision	283
Thank You!	291
Daily Affirmations	293
My Personal Journey ~ Ann Emerson	299
My Personal Journey ~ Bo Lockwood	303
Acknowledgments ~ Ann Emerson	311
Acknowledgments ~ Bo Lockwood	313
Glossary	319
References	329
Trademarks	341
About the Authors	343
Trilogy Book Series	344

FOREWORD

The English language offers more than one million words we can use to communicate toward knowing ourselves and our relationship to all that's here. The 44 words carefully selected and ordered within ESSENCE, by Ann Emerson and Bo Lockwood, offer **Sleeping Souls, Seekers**, and the **Awakened** some of the best from those one million plus, from which to live a balanced life, filled with greater joy and contentment.

One of my favorite words, or "Aspects" as the authors call these precious 44, is *Connectedness*. The quote in its *Context* section, by Chief Seattle, who lived between 1786 and 1866, tells much about the usefulness and importance of words, since we are still basking in his wisdom today: "Humankind has not woven the web of life. We are but one thread within it. Whatever we do to the web, we do to ourselves. All things are bound together. All things connect."

As my connected life experience unfolds like a **Seeker** on the edge of adventure, I find our information—comprising words—critical to the beneficial advancement of all. I wonder about the perspectives we add to the global information highway, of which we are all connected. Does the information we send and receive create accord or discord?

Miraculously, we all come equipped with an internal compass, a deeply physiological one. We've all felt joy and know it well. We can feel it in Chief Seattle's words. They bring on a smile and contentment. For those wanting to experience more of that and make a beneficial difference just by being joyful here, considering the 44 Aspects of ESSENCE, along with their Contexts and Daily Affirmations, will sustain you.

Your unique internal compass is your guide. So stay alert to your joy. Within ESSENCE, whichever Aspects you find yourself drawn to, know that just by reading them you will be advancing the well-being of everything, including yourself.

Dana B. Lichtstrahl
Princeton, New Jersey

PREFACE

As of 2017, human existence is at a precarious point in history. Overall, our awareness is low and our perspective is narrow. Most of us are living in a state of constriction, continually experiencing worry, drama, and fear.

Power, greed, and control rule our existence through oppression. The richest 1% keeps getting richer, while a majority of the world's population lives in a state of scarcity, struggling for its families' survival. The Souls of most humans are asleep.

Through expanding our self-awareness, our perspective broadens, and we view Mother Earth and ourselves in a new way. As our perspective broadens, our sleeping Souls awaken, inspiring us to disconnect from the old-paradigm story of constrictive, 20th-century living; discovering our truth and power to choose a new-paradigm story of eXpansive, 21st-century living—experiencing much greater love, joy, freedom, abundance, and peace.

This book is about how we can expand the way we view ourselves, inspiring us to establish an egalitarian world. This book is a catalyst for birthing a new human existence that lives in harmony, balance, and peace with ourselves and all of Nature.

INTRODUCTION

"When the Earth is ravaged and the animals are dying, a new tribe of people shall come unto the Earth from many colors, classes, creeds, and who by their actions and deeds shall make the Earth green again. They will be known as the warriors of the rainbow."
~ **Native American Indian Prophecy**

ESSENCE expands our self-awareness, broadens our perspective, awakens our inspiration, and unleashes our power from within. Inspiration is energy in action. Through taking inspired action, we are able to traverse to a new life in the 21st century, filled with love, joy, freedom, abundance, and peace.

To traverse means to cross a hill or mountain by means of a series of sideways movements from one line of ascent or descent to another. In relation to our personal journeys, the series of countless challenges that occur in our lives represents the mountain. Our response to these challenges determines whether we ascend or descend on our climb. Throughout our climb, there are many instances of uncertainty, and our response to this uncertainty is contingent upon our perspective as well as many other Aspects, including our levels of faith, belief, bravery, perseverance, fortitude, gratitude, and humility.

A paradigm is a typical example, pattern, or model. A perspective is a particular way of regarding something, or a point of view. Therefore, traversing to a new life in the 21st century means to embrace a new story (or model), which requires greater self-awareness as well as an infinite perspective (or point of view) for living a peaceful life on Mother Earth.

Inspiration is the opposite of empowerment. To empower is to give someone the authority to do something. This means that when we are empowered, it is contingent upon someone else doing something for us. Whereas, inspiration awakens from within, so we are not reliant on any outside people to give us the power that already resides in our Souls.

The mass of the world population is currently trapped in the constrictive, old-paradigm story of 20th-century living. This old-paradigm story is filled with fear, power, control, greed, and limitations, as well as a host of other negative aspects, all of which hold the masses of the population captive to their drama-filled lives. By living in this paradigm, one's awareness is extremely low and perspective extremely narrow.

Conversely, the eXpansive, new-paradigm story of 21st-century living comprises viewing the world we live in from a new, infinite perspective. This refreshing and limitless perspective enables us to change our story, living lives filled with love, joy, freedom, abundance, and peace. By living in this paradigm, one's awareness is extremely high and perspective extremely broad.

The mass consciousness reflects our current reality on Earth, which is plagued with old-paradigm beliefs that create war, separation, inequality, oppression, materialism, and more. By collectively choosing a new-paradigm story, the mass consciousness will traverse by creating a new vision for human existence reflective of our current level of evolution. Through union, we have the ability, consciousness, technology, and perseverance to manifest this higher-dimensional vision into our three-dimensional reality.

ESSENCE brings forth timely information for the mass world population—those stuck in the old-paradigm story—to quickly choose to gain a new sense of hope that changing their drama-filled, fear-based life is possible.

ESSENCE expands people's awareness and broadens their perspective to live a new story, one that reflects a peaceful 21st-century life. It defines the new paradigm of 21st-century living by identifying 44 Aspects to embrace if one is truly committed to building a new life. Respect is the underpinning of every Aspect—respect for one's Self, each other, Mother Earth, and the Universe. Respect is everything.

ESSENCE captures just enough depth to provide a gateway to desire to seek more. It embraces the infinite unfolding of ourselves and creates a new lens through which we can change our lives, to see the world we live in with renewed clarity.

ESSENCE is laid out in a simple format. Each Aspect of the new paradigm is defined, with each Aspect representing its own section. And each section is broken into four parts:

1. The ESSENCE of the Aspect is distilled down to its most basic definition.
2. The *Context* of the Aspect provides a deeper understanding, enabling you to quickly "get it."
3. The *Daily Affirmation* supports this Aspect of your new life through integrating it into your new daily practice, embedding this new belief into your subconscious mind.
4. The *Reflections* section provides an area at the end of each Aspect to journal any of your insights. These insights will be helpful in developing your new personal vision, reflecting your new story of 21st-century living. This new vision is an exercise that occurs once you've digested the 44 Aspects.

Immediately following the 44 Aspects, the Decision Time section describes that in May 2017, we faced a fork in the road. Many Americans didn't see this fork and have kept plodding along on the constrictive path until this very day. Now, armed with this new information, people can decide if taking a bridge to the eXpansive path is right for them. If so, then reading the second book in the ESSENCE Trilogy Book Series, *Regenerating Humanity*, may be an excellent next step for you to consider.

The process of regenerating humanity begins with each person taking responsibility for their lives, no longer relying on outside sources (government, corporations, banks, schools, etc.) to fix their problems. Remaining stuck in the old story of suffering or embracing the new story of freedom is simply a choice every one of us makes.

Arlene Rose Curley, intuitive leader and spiritual mentor, states in her book, *Completing the Seven*:

> When you inhaled that divine fiery spark at birth, your Soul was actually buried within your body's physical density and heavier earthly vibrations. It was shocked into spiritual amnesia, and within this deep sleep all the knowledge from previous lifetimes and from the heavenly spheres also went into hibernation. Thus, you began life as an ordinary being: awareness of body, mind, spirit—but no awareness of your Soul! You are born into a major predicament. Here you are on Earth, with your body housing your sleeping Soul. You have no idea that you have a Soul, and with your spiritual amnesia, you have forgotten everything.

The objective of the ESSENCE is to be a catalyst in awakening people's sleeping Souls, traversing to the new paradigm of 21st-century living.

Before beginning your journey into the depths of your Soul, it's imperative to establish a baseline measure of your current level of awakening by taking the **ESSENCE Assessment (EA44)**. You will be encouraged to take it again once you've digested the 44 Aspects, reflecting the level of personal awakening that has occurred in you as a result of reading this book. Please note that you can take this assessment as often as you desire, as you continue your seeking beyond this book, tracking your progress to a state of awakening.

Take the **ESSENCE Assessment (EA44)** now:

21stCenturyParadigm.com/ESSENCE-Assessment/

Record your results here:

Round of Results	Total Points (Out of 220)	Awakening % (Out of 100%)
Round One Results		

Now that you've established your baseline measure of awakening, you are ready to embark on this journey to awakening your Soul. This journey to awakening begins with expanding your self-awareness. . . .

Introduction

A Parable about....
Expanding Self-Awareness,
Awakening Inspiration,
Unleashing Our Power From Within
[Inspired by Dana B. Lichtstrahl]

A student is standing in front of a chalkboard, staring intently at a problem that is directly in front of their face. They are so close to the problem that all they see is the problem.

Their awareness is low, their perspective is narrow, and their frustration is overwhelming them. They don't know how to solve this problem, as they don't see any potential solutions. Standing behind them is the teacher and a classroom of students, wondering, and some even judging, what the student will do to solve this problem.

The teacher asks the student, "How do you feel?" The student mumbles, "Nervous and frustrated."

Fortunately, the teacher is aware, and knows how to inspire. They are aware that by expanding the perspective of the student, potential solutions will appear, and their frustration will be replaced by inspiration. So they asked the student to go the back of the classroom, envisioning themselves standing in front of the chalkboard, staring at the problem.

The teacher states, "By standing at the back of the classroom, you have expanded your awareness, and are now in a place of Observership which involves intent listening. Can you see yourself standing at the chalkboard?"

The student immediately replies, "Yes!"

ESSENCE

The teacher continues, "The greatest power that humans have over all other species is our ability to observe ourselves in any given situation, listening intently to those around us, while allowing our internal voice to guide us. Through expanding our self-awareness, we are in a position to appropriately RESPOND to any situation in a state of calmness and inspiration, while not REACTING to it with nervousness and frustration—for this REACTION occurs only when we are standing directly in front of the chalkboard in a state of fear."

The teacher then asks, "By standing at the back of the classroom, what else do you see?"

The student replies, "I see a lot more. I see you and all the students staring at me trying to solve the problem on the board. I see myself nervously staring at the problem on the board. I see the floor, walls, ceiling, lights, and windows. Through the windows, I see birds, grass, trees and the sky."

The teacher responds, "So your perspective is much more eXpansive from the back of the classroom. Would you agree?"

The student smiles, "Oh yes, so much more eXpansive."

The teacher probes, "So with this eXpansive perspective, do you believe there are more options available to you now, including options to solve your problem?"

The student confidently replies, "Definitely."

The teacher then asks, "So through the realization that more options are now available to you, how do you feel?"

INTRODUCTION

The student confidently states, "Calm and inspired!"

The teacher smiles wide. "So what have you learned about yourself?"

The student confirms, "I've learned about the power of expanding my self-awareness to broaden my perspective, entering a space of Observership. I've learned that by being in a place of Observership, I can view myself in any situation. I've learned that by viewing myself in a given situation, I am able to intently listen to those around me, as well as listen to my own internal voice. I've learned that by listening intently, I become more and more aware of what is going on around me. Through this elevated awareness, I am better equipped, and see more options, to solving my problem at hand. And, by having more options, a sense of calmness fills my body, while my frustration subsides and my sense of inspiration awakens."

The teacher exclaims, "YES! you just learned a very important lesson of expanding self-awareness, awakening inspiration, unleashing your power from within! You are worthy. You are powerful. You are able to inspire yourself and others, including me."

The student shines as they return to their seat.

Aspect #1

ESSENCE:

**As my self-awareness expands,
my perspective broadens.**

"We are not human beings having a spiritual experience. We are spiritual beings having a human experience."
~ **Teilhard de Chardin**

SELF-AWARENESS is the conscious knowledge of one's own character, feelings, motives, and desires, which dictates our perspective on life. The expansion of mind and heart is limitless. The greater our awareness, the greater our aliveness. The key to expanding our awareness is acquiring wisdom through learning the needed lessons of our daily challenges. With greater wisdom, we broaden our perspective, creating greater aliveness.

By having high levels of awareness (a.k.a. eXpansive awareness), we are inspired with unlimited vision and unshakable faith and belief. It is then that we have the willingness to become our vision and dream.

The following graphic clearly depicts the correlations among awareness, expansion, and perspective. Each dot represents the expansiveness of our awareness; the white arc represents our ascension, or traverse; and the angled lines represent the extensiveness of our perspective. You'll notice that the arc gets farther away from the Earth as we ascend, expanding our awareness and broadening our perspective.

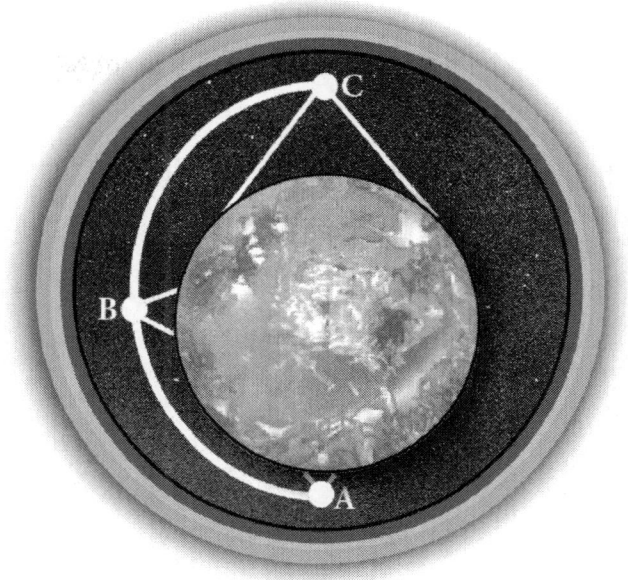

POINT A represents the **Sleeping Soul**, who is trapped in old-paradigm 20th-century living, where the mass of the world's population resides. This person's awareness is extremely low, and their perspective is extremely narrow, and they have yet to ascend to any significant degree. His or her life is filled with drama, fear, worries, doubt, insecurity, and other negative emotions. Such a life keeps going in circles.

POINT B represents the **Seeker**, who is traversing to the new paradigm of 21st-century living. There is uncertainty, yet this person is discovering calm in the unknown. His or her awareness is expanding, perspective broadening, and fear, drama, worries, doubt, and insecurity waning. Such a person is beginning to feel more inner peace and love in their life.

POINT C represents the **Awakened**, who is living in the new paradigm, viewing the world with unlimited vision, being open to all possibilities. He or she realizes they are a spiritual being having a human experience. Such a life is filled with love, joy, freedom, abundance, and peace. And this person views himself or herself as an aspect of the infinite. . . .

SELF-AWARENESS

*I view the world through an
extremely broad perspective.*

Aspect #2

ESSENCE:

I am an infinite being.

CONTEXT

"I know this world is ruled by infinite intelligence. Everything that surrounds us—everything that exists—proves that there are infinite laws behind it. There can be no denying this fact. It is mathematical in its precision."
~ Thomas A. Edison

INFINITE BEING is limitless or endless in space, extent, or size, and impossible to measure or calculate. Infinite existence produces infinite opportunity. When the greater knowledge of the infinite comes to us, we are changed forever, as all limitations are released.

Accepting that we are infinite beings validates our faith, belief, and trust in the Divine order of life. Accessing the infinite expands our imagination to new heights of creativity while we acknowledge the infinite unfolding of ourselves.

Sleeping Souls generally don't dwell on the fact that the Universe is infinite. They tend to be stuck in their ways, convinced their belief system, whereby separateness and the finite govern the Earth, is accurate. They tend to believe that they are limited to this singular life in which they are currently living. They are limited in abilities and/or opportunities to grow. They tend to overlook that their finite thinking and beliefs are holding them hostage to their current ways of living. For some, this brings comfort in security; for others, it creates a cyclone of limitation, and they cannot see any way out. Some begin to seek.

Seekers tend to be discovering the Universe in which the Earth and everything on it lives. Many are beginning to access the infinite aspects of their minds and hearts. As they ascend, discovering the Universal truths, many will no longer feel comfortable subscribing to the old-paradigm beliefs they once had.

Awakened are those who undoubtedly believe in the infinite, freeing them from the shackles of limitation. They are able to see with unlimited vision, remaining open to all possibilities. They tend to be very creative, accessing their infinite imaginations to make new discoveries, develop new ideas, and conceive new solutions to challenges. They tend to believe firmly that with vision everything is possible and everything is solvable. Most of them no longer fear dying in this chapter of their infinite life. Since they don't fear dying, they are able to live life without fear. They generally believe that the objective of each chapter of life is to learn from the challenges they experience, apply this knowledge through the accumulation of wisdom, expand their awareness, broaden their perspective, and awaken to the fulfillment of their life's purpose. And, through their infinite belief system, they realize that everything is connected. . . .

*I am an infinite being accepting
from an infinite source.*

Aspect #3

ESSENCE:

I am connected with the Universe.

CONTEXT

"Humankind has not woven the web of life. We are but one thread within it. Whatever we do to the web, we do to ourselves. All things are bound together. All things connect."
~ Chief Seattle

CONNECTEDNESS is to bring things together or into contact so that a real or notional link is established. It is a spiritual belief; that is, it goes beyond the physical realm. Every aspect of the infinite Universe is connected, negating the illusion of separateness. As John Donne wrote in the late 17th century, "No man is an island," as we all depend upon, affect, and are influenced by Nature and the Universe. We are One, made of the same matter, learning the same lessons, desiring joy-filled and peaceful lives.

Sleeping Souls generally don't realize that everyone and everything is connected. They tend not to understand that the way in which we treat the Earth is a reflection of how we treat ourselves. Without this connection to Mother Earth intact, they tend to rush to profit at the expense of the environment. Their lives tend to involve separateness, discrimination, judgment, and inequality. Most tend to believe that the circumstances in their lives are out of their control. Consequently, they tend to believe that they are the victims of these circumstances, while all along not realizing they are the cause of them. They simply don't see the connection. Some begin to seek.

Seekers tend to begin to make the connection between their thoughts, ideas, behaviors, actions, and how these attributes form the lives they live. As they begin to discover connectedness, many will be thirsty for more information. Many will gain a clearer understanding of quantum physics, a science that explains how everything in our world comes into existence and validates the idea that everything is connected. As a result, they learn how to leverage quantum physics to manifest their life by design instead of by default.

Awakened tend to know that everything is connected. They discard the illusion of separateness and tend to respect other humans and the Earth in the same way they desire to be respected. They tend to deeply understand how and why their thoughts, ideas, behaviors, and actions control the outcome of their lives. And, through their understanding of connectedness, they also tend to understand that everything works in balance. . . .

CONNECTEDNESS

*I am connected as One with
all aspects of the Universe.*

_____

_____

_____

_____

_____

_____

Aspect #4

ESSENCE:

Accurate information creates balance in my life.

CONTEXT

*"Happiness is not a matter of intensity
but of balance and order and rhythm and harmony."*

~ **Thomas Merton**

BALANCE is an even distribution of weight, enabling someone or something to remain upright and steady. Balance is a Universal truth —the yin and yang of all existence. "As above, so below" is a statement of spiritual balance. Without balance, our lives are filled with drama and poor decisions.

As humans, we are a perfect aspect of creation. However, most of us don't know this and instead believe subconsciously that we are limited beings. Falsely believing that we are never enough can prompt us to overcompensate. For instance, we may work too hard, or possess more than we can properly care for. This puts us into a state of imbalance. Since Nature is inherently balanced, we are then living out of harmony with it.

Sleeping Souls generally don't consider the balance of life, Nature, and the Earth. They understand the smaller, basic elements of balance—male/female, up/down, in/out, good/bad—but they tend not to grasp the larger balance of the integrated whole system of the Earth and the Universe. Many tend subconsciously to believe this inaccurate information about their place in the Universe, creating an inner imbalance that affects their ability to live in harmony with Mother Earth. As a result, many tend to be living a constrictive life filled with fear, doubt, worries, drama, and insecurity. This inaccurate information is often handed down from generation to generation, until one day it gets called into question. Some begin to seek.

Seekers begin to grasp that we as humans are perfect, although our actions, decisions, and behaviors are imperfect when the information in our subconscious minds is inaccurate. Many begin questioning the accuracy of their limiting beliefs through deep introspection. They learn that the conscious mind is a gatekeeper, protecting the information in the subconscious mind without understanding its accuracy. Some learn to re-program their subconscious minds with accurate information comprising new beliefs. Through this transformation, many tend to accept and forgive themselves and others.

Awakened tend to be living in balance with themselves and in harmony with Mother Earth. By having accurate information in their subconscious minds, they have expanded their awareness and broadened their perspective, knowing that their life extends well beyond bodily existence. And many realize that living in balance with all aspects of the Earth and the Universe begins to resemble what is known as regenerative living. . . .

BALANCE

*With accurate information,
I live harmoniously in balance.*

Aspect #5

ESSENCE:

Regenerative living enables me to be in harmony with Nature and myself.

CONTEXT

*"Let us not seek the Republican answer
or the Democratic answer, but the right answer.
Let us not seek to fix the blame for the past.
Let us accept our own responsibility for the future."*
~ **John F. Kennedy**

REGENERATIVE describes the action and/or process of regenerating or being regenerated. Regenerative living is the transitional action and process leading to 21st-century living filled with love, joy, freedom, abundance, and peace.

Humanity is in need of being regenerated: spiritually, physically, psychologically, emotionally, and economically. Therefore, regenerative living is a reflection of awakening our Souls and is the path we can choose to follow. Taking this path is not for convenience; rather, it's a matter of survival. At its essence, regenerative is analogous to the Japanese term *kaizen*, which means continuous improvement.

As humans on Earth, we possess the ability to live in absolute harmony with each other and all of Nature. What stands in the way are the old-paradigm beliefs, ideas, behaviors, and actions that continue to literally destroy the Earth. Regenerative living is the outgrowth of living sustainably, because we cannot afford to sustain the constrictive path we are on until it leads us to extinction.

Sleeping Souls generally have little concern for how their behaviors and actions affect the next seven generations. Their constrictive consciousness has them caught up in their self-centered lives. They are so consumed by the drama of today that they cannot see tomorrow. Their narrow perspective of the world limits their ability to see the future, which is being destroyed by their current-day actions. Some begin to seek.

Seekers are beginning to wake up to the reality of our times. Their perspective has broadened to realize that the path we are on does lead to extinction. Most want to make a difference in our world by shifting this trajectory in a new direction—one that will lead to living in harmony, not in competition, with Nature.

Awakened tend to know firmly that our global community needs to regenerate, that is, to bring about a renewed existence. They realize that if balance and peace on Earth are to exist, then the world's population needs to drop old core beliefs, habits and limitations, clear its minds of negativity, and cleanse the feelings that create separateness. Their awareness is that, in the past 200 years, humans have created more devastation and degradation to the environment than at any other time in history. Many realize that regenerative living means living in balance with all aspects of the Earth, which will occur through learning. . . .

I live in harmony with Nature, for I am Nature.

_____

_____

_____

_____

_____

Aspect #6

ESSENCE:

I am a lifelong learner.

CONTEXT

"I like a teacher who gives you something to take home to think about besides homework."
~ **Lily Tomlin as Edith Ann, *Sesame Street***

LEARNING is the acquisition of knowledge or skills through experience, practice, study, or being taught. Learning is essential to our development. To be human is to desire to learn. By the time a baby reaches three months old, its desire to learn is evident. At the core of our Souls, there is a strong desire for us to keep learning and to acquire wisdom.

Sleeping Souls tend to describe themselves as being stuck in a continuous vortex of drama, as the same things keep happening to them over and over again. Perhaps they are failing to realize that this is occurring because they are not capturing the ESSENCE of the learning. As a result, they tend to continue to go in circles, and as they do, the lessons become harder and harder. Some are so stuck in their ways—driven by their need to be right—that they lead themselves directly into an emotional breakdown. It is then that many experience being hit over the head with a spiritual two-by-four. Some begin to seek.

Seekers tend to be learning that, to awaken our Souls and ascend, we need to acquire wisdom. Learning creates wisdom through responding to challenges in life. Seekers tend to realize that if they don't learn from the experience, it will undoubtedly repeat itself in the future. Whereas, if they capture the learning from the experience, then they grow, and the negative energy they encountered is released to the Universe to be utilized productively elsewhere.

Awakened tend to believe that regenerative living involves continuous improvement, which depends on continuous learning. Many have adopted a knowing that "experiences in life happen for us, not to us." Therefore, they view themselves as students of life, not victims of life. They also tend to see that wisdom is acquired through learning, and that learning is acquired through life experiences. As Tony Robbins states, "I've come to believe that all my past failures and frustration were actually laying the foundation for the understandings that have created the new level of living I now enjoy." Tony has certainly acquired a lot of wisdom in his life. . . .

LEARNING

I continue to learn throughout my lifetime.

———————————————

———————————————

———————————————

———————————————

———————————————

Aspect #7

ESSENCE:

**As I acquire wisdom,
I evolve and the Universe evolves.**

"To make no mistake is not in the power of man; but from their errors and mistakes the wise and good learn wisdom for the future."

~ Plutarch

WISDOM is the quality of having experience, knowledge, and good judgment; it is the state of being wise. Wisdom is essential to our evolution. Wisdom is gained by learning through the challenges of life's experiences. All challenges are potential wisdom makers. As we gain wisdom, we evolve our Souls.

Sleeping Souls tend to have extremely low awareness and avoid discomfort at all costs. When they continuously avoid discomfort, they live life in denial. Living in denial is not an authentic way to live. Rather, it's more like a fairyland in Hell, in that to the outside world they have successfully created an illusion that their lives are perfect, while all along, their Soul is in turmoil. For many, until they face their fears, learning the lessons and capturing the wisdom, nothing will change. Some begin to seek.

Seekers tend to embrace discomfort because they are beginning to realize that discomfort is our higher Selves informing us that a lesson from the challenge at hand needs to be learned. They realize that discomfort leads them to their center of knowing. And when they acknowledge, accept, and integrate this learning into their lives, the negative energy releases and the discomfort dissipates. In other words, they discover comfort in the discomfort because they know there is wisdom to be gained. However, if they don't capture the learning or if they deny the discomfort, this uncomfortable challenge will return again in the future. This is why many of them embrace discomfort, as they are on a journey to take on as many challenges as possible to ascend to a state of awakening.

Awakened tend to believe that our Souls experience one infinite life, comprising an infinite number of chapters. Within each chapter we gain wisdom. And the wisdom gained along the way determines how consciously evolved their Souls are. Hence, the term *old Soul* recognizes an individual as consciously evolved through already having experienced numerous chapters of their infinite life. They tend to acknowledge the opportunity within every lesson learned, to have earned knowledge through learning the lesson, and to give thanks for all lessons no matter how difficult. By having this awareness about learning and wisdom, they tend to awaken to their life's purpose. . . .

WISDOM

*I rely on my wisdom to make
the proper choices in life.*

———————————————

———————————————

———————————————

———————————————

———————————————

———————————————

Aspect #8

ESSENCE:

My life's purpose aligns with my true heart's desires.

"We ourselves feel that what we are doing is just a drop in the ocean. But the ocean would be less because of that missing drop."
~ **Mother Teresa**

PURPOSE is the reason for which something is done or created, or for which something exists. Purpose leads us to authentic happiness in life. According to Bikram Choudhury, an Indian yoga teacher, as long as we are still breathing, our life's purpose has not yet been fulfilled. Discovering our life's purpose is a journey, and it's the Seeker who happens to find it.

Spiritual chaplain Lisa Gruenloh describes our purpose as "the aspect of us that is completely passionate about helping others in purposeful ways. Our passion helps us to identify our life's purpose. Then, by connecting with our higher Selves, we are effortlessly guided by our intuition through inspired action."

Sleeping Souls tend to snicker at the notion of having a life's purpose. They write it off as religious nonsense. Rather, they get sucked into the illusion of success, which at the core is about gaining prestige, power, control, and money. They tend to believe the level of success they achieve is reflected by where they live, the size of their houses, the types of cars they drive, the schools their children attend, and the title on their business cards. Their conditional programming drives them to "keep up with the Joneses," which leads them to purchasing all of this materialistic stuff, only to, most likely, discover that they are not authentically happy. An internal uneasiness eats away at them, and yet they can't pinpoint the source of this discomfort. Some begin to seek.

Seekers tend to make tremendous progress in their journey when they discover and embrace their life's purpose. For many, materialism becomes secondary and simplicity becomes primary. For many, their competitive nature transitions to a collaborative one. Their self-centeredness is replaced with compassion for others; drama subsides and inner peace ensues, and faith replaces fear as they serve their life's purpose.

Awakened tend to believe that when they live their life's purpose, their mission will be achieved and they will ascend to a higher dimension in the next chapter of their infinite life. They tend not to allow success to go to their heads, as they are simply following their life's purpose. And if they don't achieve their purpose, thus gaining the level of wisdom needed to ascend, they will return to this same level of consciousness in their next chapter. Many believe their life's purpose involves creating positive change here on Earth. . . .

PURPOSE

I am fulfilled by serving my life's purpose.

_____

_____

_____

_____

_____

Aspect #9

ESSENCE:

**I make changes in my life
to live a story worth telling.**

*"The decisions you make today,
determine the stories you tell tomorrow."*
~ **Craig Groeschel**

CHANGE is to make or become different. Change is constant in life. "We cannot step into the same river twice." If we view change as positive, we discover that new pathways are always available, earning us the right to enter a new facet of life.

Our society is plagued with a limiting belief that affirms, "Accept each other for who we are because people don't change that much." The "acceptance" aspect is true; however, the "don't change" aspect is not true. By the time we are teenagers, we undoubtedly have a blueprint of our core beliefs firmly embedded in our subconscious minds. This blueprint is our operating system that guides us through life. However, at some point in life when we challenge this blueprint of beliefs, we may be ready to change ourselves.

Sleeping Souls tend to be stuck in their ways, highly resistant to change, because they find it difficult to question their existing belief system. They live in fear, mainly fear of themselves. As a result, many of them never take the time to truly challenge their core beliefs, because if they did, they would discover that many of them are inaccurate. And as people get older, they find it increasingly difficult to accept that they have been living with constrictive ideas and behaviors, blocking full aliveness. Even when people realize that their subconscious thinking is flawed, they often do not know how to reprogram their subconscious minds to reflect the accuracy of their newly discovered truths. Some begin to seek.

Seekers tend to challenge everything, although in their past they've tried to figure it out, only to come up empty. They tend to learn from others who have gone before them, realizing that figuring out an infinite Universe is impossible. Therefore, their change comes through accepting the great mystery of life. In order to accept the unknown, you must have faith. And through having faith, Seekers tend to make tremendous strides in their personal evolution.

Awakened tend to know without doubt that the higher realms support those who have faith. Their belief in God, the Divine energy source, is unwavering. For those who were once Sleeping Souls now see the world and the Universe from an eXpansive perspective. They fully accept that no one can stop life's movement and therefore view change as a way to keep evolving infinitely. They have learned that true change occurs when they transition to a heart-centered life. . . .

CHANGE

*I am open to, and accept, all changes
that support my life's purpose.*

Aspect #10

ESSENCE:

I consistently move my ego from my mind to my heart.

CONTEXT

"It is better in prayer to have a heart without words than words without a heart."
~ Mahatma Gandhi

HEART-CENTEREDNESS puts the heart at the focal point of one's life. Heart-centeredness enables us to live peacefully and harmoniously with Nature, the Universe, and ourselves. As a result, our thoughts, ideas, behaviors, actions, and love originate from our hearts, not our minds.

In our life's journey, the longest distance to travel is the 12 inches between our mind and heart. Westernized conditioning has embedded in our collective consciousness that we should lead with our minds, trying to figure out life's challenges, imposing our egos and personal will to get the outcomes we desire. This thinking is flawed, as evident by our current state of global affairs. It's time we move our egos out of our minds and into our hearts.

Sleeping Souls generally have closed their hearts. Fear is keeping them closed, as many fear rejection if they dare to truly love another. Societal programming views love as a jail sentence because it's a loss of freedom and control. A controlling mind cannot coexist with a loving heart. People's need to control others stems from their own fears and insecurities about themselves and represents clear evidence of a closed heart. The greatest crimes, fear, and hatred all come from closed hearts. Sleeping Souls tend to view the world through a perspective of separateness, which is a reflection of living in the mind and not in the heart. Separateness fuels wars, discrimination, religious differences, judgment, resistance, inequality, and a host of other negative attributes. The illusion of separateness is a form of oppression because the best way to control a society is to separate it. This illusion is clearly reflected in America and many other regions of the world at this time. Some begin to seek.

Seekers tend to be traversing from a mind-centered to a heart-centered life. They tend to be viewing the Earth with eXpansive awareness, vastly broadening their perspective. This new perspective enables them to let go of fears, the illusion of separateness, and other limiting beliefs. They choose to change their stories, living heart-centered lives.

Awakened tend to have successfully moved their egos out of their minds and into their hearts. Many have rid themselves of any skepticism, thereby fully trusting their hearts to naturally guide them in the right direction. They realize that if being heart-centered poses a challenge, then it is likely that forgiveness may be in order. . . .

HEART-CENTEREDNESS

*I live a heart-centered life,
making heart-centered decisions.*

_____

_____

_____

_____

_____

_____

Aspect #11

ESSENCE:

Forgiveness is one of my greatest strengths.

CONTEXT

*"I can forgive, but I cannot forget,
is only another way of saying, I will not forgive.
Forgiveness ought to be like a cancelled note—torn in two,
and burned up, so that it never be shown against one."*

~ Henry Ward Beecher

FORGIVENESS is the action or process of forgiving or being forgiven. Forgiveness is one of our greatest strengths. We tend to think that forgiveness is mainly for others; however, it is really for ourselves. It's amazing how drama in our lives quickly dissipates when forgiveness is in our hearts. Letting go of past hurts and resentments enables us to be fully present, positioning us to maximize our human potential.

Learning forgiveness is among the more difficult challenges we face on our quest for ascension. Nonetheless, once we reach a certain altitude—leaving the drama at base camp—forgiveness simply becomes a new way of life. We learn through forgiveness to release the negative energies holding us captive to ourselves: anger, envy, jealousy, resentment, and perhaps even hatred.

Sleeping Souls tend to be rather weak in the area of forgiveness. Many remain stuck in their stories, clutching onto negative energy, gossiping to others, justifying why they are victims. A victim mentality has a very low energetic vibration, thus attracting like-frequency experiences into people's lives. Then they wonder why their lives are full of fear, doubt, worries, drama, and insecurity. A lack of forgiveness is often passed on from generation to generation. Some begin to seek.

Seekers tend to learn that forgiveness is a key that all of us possess that unlocks a door to mental freedom. When our minds are filled with negative thoughts, there is no room for new, vibrant thought-forms to enter. They learn that true forgiveness releases these low-vibrating frequencies of energy. While remembering their history, they are making room for the magical essence of spirit to fill this newly created space. They realize forgiveness must be authentic and pure, with the understanding that any form of future abuse will not be tolerated.

Awakened tend to understand that all of us are teachers for one another, and that life experiences happen for us and not to us. They realize that every single human being makes mistakes and has regrets. The difference resides in whether they can forgive themselves. They tend to know that carrying guilt and shame around eats away at their aliveness, drains energy from their cells, and holds them back from realizing their full potential. Guilt and shame are very low energetic vibrations, while releasing these negative emotions improves their well-being tremendously. And they tend to know that forgiveness contributes greatly to Self-love. . . .

FORGIVENESS

I forgive myself and others, as we are all teachers for one another. Forgiveness is my path to freedom.

Aspect #12

ESSENCE:

I love myself.

CONTEXT

"Loving myself has been such a challenge."
~ Alison Stormwolf

SELF-LOVE is an intense feeling of deep affection for one's Self. Self-love is where love originates. Old-paradigm belief is that Self-love is selfish and narcissistic. This is absolutely not true. New-paradigm belief is that there is no guilt or shame in Self-love, there is only love.

Sleeping Souls tend to live in their minds, not in their hearts, to figure out what they need. As a result, their love for others can be rather empty and is often a manipulation to get love or attention in an attempt to fill their void. Relying on others to fill them with love, while being incapable of returning the love because of their closed hearts, simply doesn't work. Dependency on others to fill themselves with love is a recipe for disaster. Many don't realize that they cannot deeply care for and love another until they love themselves. For example, many women are lacking in Self-love due to limiting beliefs that they learned in the old paradigm, which has them believing that they are not good enough and therefore subordinated and unworthy. Many men are lacking in Self-love due to their hearts being closed, as they have been conditioned in the old paradigm to believe that feelings and crying are only for sissies. Many Sleeping Souls fail to realize that the love they are yearning for already resides within them. Some begin to seek.

Seekers tend to learn that centeredness and calmness can't exist without love and that the key to unleashing love in their life begins with Self-love. When Self-love is unleashed, they are inspired, embracing their authentic selves, increasing their confidence, self-esteem, and independence. They forgive and accept themselves. Many come to discover that if there are attributes of themselves that they don't love, they have the power to simply choose a new story, because "the decisions they make today, determine the stories they tell tomorrow." They realize there is no better time to change their life than the present time.

Awakened generally realize that a solid foundation for a relationship exists when two confident, independent people, both filled with Self-love, unite. They are together because they each desire to be together, not because they need to be together. This brings about relationships based on love and equality, which are also ingredients required for world peace. Many believe that Self-love means rediscovering the heart as their home. This is about embracing and loving their true, authentic Selves, enabling them to be secure and centered while owning the joy of life without denial. As they embrace Self-love, they feel God within. . . .

SELF-LOVE

I love myself infinitely.

_____

_____

_____

_____

_____

_____

Aspect #13

ESSENCE:

There is a spark of God within me.

*"We shall serve for the joy of serving,
prosperity shall flow to us and through us
in unending streams of plenty."*
~ Charles Fillmore

GOD WITHIN is a belief that there's a spark of God within each and every one of us. "I see God in you" is a spiritual statement supporting this belief. Because every atom in our Universe is filled with energy, and since God is the Divine energy source, then there is a spark of God in every aspect of the Universe—including ourselves.

Many old-paradigm religions have convinced their congregations to believe that God is out there and the only way to enlightenment is through their respective religious institution. It has been a strategy through which many religious institutions control their members and take their money while imposing fear, guilt, and shame onto their congregations.

Moreover, this belief is not true. Rather, God's spark of energy resides within each person regardless of religious sect, age, gender, race, sexual preference, or socioeconomic status. God is energy, and our personal energetic vibration reflects how we relate with this Divine energy.

Sleeping Souls carry the spark of God without ever realizing it. Therefore, many are not tapping into this infinite energy source. Many will only pray out of need, and when God doesn't respond in a way that they recognize, they validate in their minds that God doesn't exist. What they fail to realize is that God doesn't respond to need, because God has already provided us with an infinite Universe. What more can God provide than infinite possibility? Some begin to seek.

Seekers generally learn to get out of their conscious minds and into their hearts, helping to open up the intuition, creativity and knowing that every human possesses. They tend to learn that all the answers we seek already reside within ourselves, as it is through our hearts (and subconscious minds) that we connect with the Divine source of infinite opportunity. Many of them learn that creativity unleashes their ability to be a cocreator of the Universe.

Awakened tend to have unwavering faith and belief in God, which enables them to stop trying to figure out why and how everything works and instead listen to and trust the guidance from within. The future is always bright for those who trust who they are and their ability to create in the present. They fully believe that they are cocreators of the Universe. And by tapping into the God within, their Soul awakens, discovering a great sense of pervading honesty within their hearts. . . .

GOD WITHIN

I am connected to God within me.

Aspect #14

ESSENCE:

I live my life with honesty.

CONTEXT

"A half truth is a whole lie."
~**Yiddish Proverb**

HONESTY is the act of being free of deceit and untruthfulness. Honesty is the quality of being genuine and uncorrupted. Honesty is reflected through our speech, behaviors and thoughts.

Honesty through our speech is speaking our truth with sincerity, not lying or deceiving. Honesty through our behaviors is being upright and fair in our dealings with others, neither cheating nor stealing, not deceiving others by the way we act (such as making things appear to be one way when they are in fact different), without façade or hypocrisy. Honesty through our thoughts is not deceiving ourselves, nor is it believing we are fooling Spirit.

Honesty begins with being honest with ourselves. Do we live our lives with absolute truthfulness? Do we take responsibility for our actions? Do we apologize to others when we hurt them? Do we forgive others who hurt us? Do we realize that partial truths are lies? Are we living our truths, or are we living our lies?

Sleeping Souls tend to live in the old paradigm, which teaches them that white lies are acceptable, and justify their actions by not wanting to hurt the other person. Some believe that they are living honest lives because they are not out stealing cars and robbing banks, even though they may pilfer supplies from work, cheat on their income taxes, and/or fudge on the time clock, not giving an honest day's work for an honest day's pay. Some are hypocrites, pretending to possess certain virtues, morals, and beliefs, when in reality they do not. Some are tired of living a life of lies. Some begin to seek.

Seekers tend to be truthful; however, they also learn that honesty is not about "letting it all hang out" and justifying their candor by claiming that they're just being totally honest. Rather, they learn that honesty in speech must be both truthful and controlled. In other words, they speak their truth in love, and they desire to support others' gifts.

Awakened remain true to themselves. They make a commitment to live with honesty and integrity. They tend not to placate others by telling them what they want to hear; nor do they attempt to convince others that they are telling the truth. By living their lives with honesty, they tend to discover an ability to stretch beyond their former capacity for living while gaining a sense of inner peace. And through living with honesty, they are able to more fully embody their authentic selves....

HONESTY

I live my life with a pure and honest heart.

Aspect #15

ESSENCE:

Authenticity enables the real me to thrive.

CONTEXT

*"Always be a first-rate version of yourself,
instead of a second-rate version of somebody else."*

~ Judy Garland

AUTHENTICITY is fully embracing our genuine selves, thus remaining true to who we really are. Authentic people are inspired, confident, independent, and calm. They seek inner direction rather than direction from the media-saturated outside world.

Many regrets in life stem from instances when we are not our authentic selves, when we are succumbing to peer pressure, placating others, going against our intuition, or following the crowd to be cool and fit in.

Peer pressure and cultural conditioning expect us to act a certain way. And that is exactly what many of us do—we act. We act a certain way when we are at work or school. We act a certain way when the boss or teacher is around. We act a certain way when attending our houses of worship. We act a certain way when we are with our friends. We act a certain way when we are with our parents and families. These are a lot of acts to keep track of! Perhaps the question one may want to consider is: In which act are you truly your authentic self?

Sleeping Souls tend not to be connected to their authentic selves. Rather, they have a tendency to succumb to peer and societal pressures pushing them to act and look a certain way. They tend to put on a show in an effort to placate others and gain acceptance. Entire communities are made up of Sleeping Souls who feel the social pressure to put aside their authentic selves and be someone they are not. They are living a lie due to their own lack of confidence and tremendous need of acceptance, prohibiting them from being who they truly are. Some begin to seek.

Seekers generally learn that placating others at the expense of dishonoring their authentic selves is no way to live. On their quest toward ascension, there is an awakening of inspiration, while an inner sense of confidence and personal wisdom expands. They open to their authentic selves, expressing their talents without self-importance, enabling them to become their personal best. They come to realize that acting is exhausting and that people simply need to accept them for who they truly are.

Awakened tend to honor reality, choosing to be aware and accepting of imperfections in themselves and others. They live their lives with integrity and tend to be open-hearted, compassionate, and friendly people. Their actions and behaviors are consistent from one social setting to the next, without concern for acceptance by others, because they have already accepted themselves. They possess the ability to live their truth. . . .

AUTHENTICITY

I inspire others by being my authentic self.

Aspect #16

ESSENCE:

Truth is my protection.

CONTEXT

"The ability to lie is a liability."
~ **Unknown**

TRUTH is that which is true or in accordance with fact or reality. Truth is our protection, meaning, as long as we live with integrity, convincing others of our truth is unnecessary. Knowing we are living our own truth is what matters most.

Living our truth is putting ourselves out in the world by following our true hearts' desires. When we follow our hearts, we follow truth. Our truth may be entering a new career, starting a business, becoming a single parent, adopting a child, sharing hidden feelings with others, or doing a multitude of other things. The truth we hold is the reflection of our hearts' greatest joys.

Sleeping Souls tend to ignore the truth their hearts naturally carry, thus setting a trap for themselves. They tend to lose sight of the original target when the joy of the heart's truth is not present, making them fall short of the goal every time. Many find themselves in careers and/or relationships that they don't want to be in, yet they are frozen in fear, not taking any action to change the situations. Many find themselves placating others' desires at the expense of sacrificing their dreams. Perhaps a student is very artistic yet is studying accounting because their father or mother is an accountant. Or perhaps a person feels stuck in an abusive, disrespectful relationship for fear of being alone and the stigma of being single. Or perhaps a couple is expecting a baby and is feeling the pressure of needing to get married. In other words, Sleeping Souls tend not to live their truths but rather spend their lives placating others. Some begin to seek.

Seekers tend to call upon their inner strength and courage so that faith in their growth process is restored by the truth that lives within them, unhindered by deceptions, illusions, and pressures of societal programming. When they feel as if the world is presenting them with conflicts that are too heavy to carry, they have a tendency to aim higher— seeking and finding the reserve of courage in their Souls and using it to honor the truth inside their hearts.

Awakened tend to simply live their truth. They have discovered their life's purpose and don't waste their energy placating others. They have discovered that the truth in life is to follow their passion, which is their higher Self guiding them to living a life of joy and creativity. They tend to live with open hearts and open minds, accepting and honoring abundance in all aspects of their lives. They have learned to trust Divine timing, trust themselves, and trust others. . . .

TRUTH

I live my truth, as it protects me.

———————————————————

———————————————————

———————————————————

———————————————————

———————————————————

Aspect #17

ESSENCE:

Trust is a prerequisite to hope.

CONTEXT

"A person who trusts no one can't be trusted."
~ **Jerome Blattner**

TRUST is the firm belief in the reliability, truth, ability, or strength of someone or something. Trusting others begins with trusting ourselves. Trust is the foundation of meaningful relationships. With trust, there is hope. With hope, there is inspiration.

Trusting ourselves involves trusting our intuition, our gut feelings. When we feel something, it is time to be introspective and determine if that feeling has validity. It is far too easy to ignore our warning systems in this hectic, modern world only to regret not having taken the time to listen and trust ourselves. Remember, we feel in our hearts, not in our minds.

Sleeping Souls have a tendency to believe that trust is something that must be earned. In other words, the natural tendency is not to trust. Perhaps this is because they don't trust themselves. It is plausible that the lack of trust in themselves may be due to living in fear, regret, guilt, and shame. Many have a tendency to trust or not trust others by the superficial-glare factor—What do they look like?

What kind of clothes do they wear? How long is their hair? Do they wear sunglasses? What kind of music do they listen to? Are they religious? They have yet to discover the untapped potential of trusting their intuition from within. Some begin to seek.

Seekers tend to learn that trusting themselves builds their strength, and strength comes from intuitive knowing and walking their truth. Many realize that when they are out of balance and their goals are unclear, it's time to go into the cave of silence, listening to themselves and trusting what they hear.

Awakened tend to trust themselves fully. They tend to view trustworthiness as one of their greatest qualities. Many have an uncanny ability to quickly assess the trustworthiness of another simply by connecting with that person's energetic vibration while using their own intuition. They have learned the importance of not listening to the opinions of most others, listening instead to their own hearts. Many have learned that each person is unique and holds a special piece to the Universal puzzle. They understand that each person is responsible for their piece of the puzzle (a.k.a. life's purpose). They trust themselves to handle and connect their own piece responsibly. They also tend to have faith in humanity's ability to find the inner answers that heal the Self and, in turn, be at One with the Self, in harmony with others and Mother Earth. They realize that trust is a prerequisite to hope. . . .

TRUST

I trust myself and others.

Aspect #18

ESSENCE:

My life is filled with hope.

CONTEXT

"Hope is the magic carpet that transport us from the present moment into the realm of infinite possibilities."
~ H. Jackson Brown, Jr.

HOPE is a feeling of expectation and desire for a certain thing to happen. Hope can change a person, a community, a country, and the world. Hope is a leading indicator of future success.

Conversely, fear is holding back the global economy. Fear has brought about a sense of hopelessness. As long as we perceive matters in this way, the economy will not get better. When we take the time to figure out our life's purpose, it brings about a sense of hope, which leads to inspiration. Inspiring through hope is critical, because until we are inspired, no meaningful actions occur. With inspiration, our creativity blossoms and we carry out our work with pride and passion. We demonstrate our pride through our passion. Our passion leads us to unleashing the infinite power from within. Until a sense of hope, inspiration, pride, and passion are instilled throughout the world, our Souls will not awaken, our potential will not flourish, and not much will change.

According to a GALLUP Poll, 95% of U.S. 5th- through 12th-graders say it is likely they will have a better life than their parents, whereas only 50% of U.S. adults age 18 and older say that. This *hope divide* is unfortunate because it might limit the support that adults are willing to give children to help them reach their full potential.

Sleeping Souls tend to feel a sense of hopelessness, as they can't see the pathway leading them out of the quagmire. Many adults believe their children are fantasizing about a future that is out of their reach. These cautions are grounded in some wisdom, but they also might be associated with their pessimism about their own future, their vulnerabilities, or their profound inability to predict the future. Many Sleeping Souls, young and old, yearn for a sense of hope. Some begin to seek.

Seekers tend to view the world differently, as they expand their awareness and acquire a renewed sense of hope. Many learn that the answers they are seeking reside within, inspiring them to action and fueling their creativity and passion. Their hope is contagious.

Awakened tend to have a zest for life, desiring to live life to the fullest. They tend to have a high degree of hope, along with an affirming belief that a shift in consciousness is approaching a global tipping point and it's simply a matter of time before the world begins to view itself through the new paradigm of 21st-century living. Their abundant hope fuels their faith. . . .

HOPE

My high degree of hope is contagious.

Aspect #19

ESSENCE:

I have faith that my intangible Spirit exists.

CONTEXT

*"Faith is taking the first step
even when you don't see the whole staircase."*
~Martin Luther King, Jr.

FAITH is complete trust or confidence in someone or something. Faith in the intangible is graceful when we live in our hearts and unstable when we live in our minds. *Having faith,* in its broadest context, simply means that we believe in the intangible aspects of life, knowing that many things exist even though we cannot see them, including our higher Selves.

Having faith is taken out of context too many times by people believing that it means *being religious*. This is another inaccurate and limiting belief. Cell phones, Wi-Fi, Bluetooth, microwaves, radio waves, and other invisible frequencies of energy obviously exist. Our spirit is no different, as this energy is the intangible aspect of ourselves.

Sleeping Souls tend to have little faith in the intangible aspects of themselves. Many tend to be living in fear, which is the opposite of living in faith. Many want and even attempt to have faith, but their minds are in contradiction to faith, and therefore, faith doesn't sustain itself in their lives. Some even pretend to have faith out of fear of not having faith. Some begin to seek.

Seekers generally learn that they can connect with their intangible Self when they get out of their minds and into their hearts. Many have come to learn that it is when they live a heart-centered life that they are connected with their higher Self. And believing in and connecting with their higher Self requires faith. They tend to learn that having faith involves letting go of old, limiting beliefs, while sharing from the heart with no strings attached. They tend be able to release anything in their life that does not apply to their present state of growth. This includes the release of old habits, acquaintances that drain them, the need for approval or recognition, and any other aspects of their life that no longer serve them. They have faith that releasing the old will make space for new experiences, new people, and new abundance.

Awakened tend to have unwavering faith. They know that being connected with their higher Self means being guided by their intuition. They tend to focus their lives by fully embracing their creativity and passion, and take action only when inspired to do so. They generally utilize their intuition to work through difficult challenges. Many tend to release the old and make way for the new by using only what they need—helping to assure abundance for the next seven generations, a main tenet of regenerative living. And many have a high degree of belief in the spiritual realm. . . .

FAITH

*I have faith that we will transition to
21st-century living, preserving Mother Earth
for the next seven generations.*

ASPECT#20

ESSENCE:

I believe in a source energy greater than myself.

"The future belongs to those who believe in the beauty of their dreams."
~ Eleanor Roosevelt

BELIEF is an acceptance that a statement is true or that something exists. Belief is powerful, as those who believe in their dreams have the ability to bring them to life.

Sleeping Souls will never reach their full potential without believing in themselves. In our current global recession, many are stuck in mind traps of scarcity, lack, and fear. These thoughts and emotions would not be holding them captive if they truly believed in themselves and were able to tap their infinite power source from within. Capable people on this Earth have the potential to improve their present-day lives. Belief, bravery, perseverance, and fortitude are among the aspects required to create positive change. Nevertheless, many Sleeping Souls will continue to make excuses, acting out the role of victim without truly considering the possibility that they are stuck in their situations due to a lack of belief in themselves. Some begin to seek.

Seekers tend to be successful in clearing out past hurts and resentments through forgiveness, establishing a renewed sense of belief in themselves. Many have released the old-paradigm beliefs in limitations, finite abilities, and unworthiness, replacing them with new-paradigm beliefs in infinite opportunities, infinite abilities, and infinite love. They tend to let go of the past, choosing to be fully aware in the present, and hopeful for the future —consciously choosing to experience a rebirth in this chapter of their lives.

Awakened tend to have successfully stepped into the infinite, believing they are cocreators of the Universe. They have masterfully let go of all past negativity, bringing forth the positive wisdom they have acquired into their new-paradigm life. Many have experienced the ecstasy of rebirth, viewing the world with unlimited vision. They are calm and centered amid the chaos of the noisy world around them. They believe in themselves because of the courage and perseverance they have shown through their spiritual quest toward a higher awareness and a broader perspective. Through being connected to the spiritual realm, many have learned to allow Divine timing to determine when the outcome will occur. . . .

BELIEF

I believe in my abilities and myself.

_____

_____

_____

_____

_____

_____

ASPECT#21

ESSENCE:

I allow Divine will to determine the outcome.

CONTEXT

*"All I have seen teaches me to trust
the Creator for all I have not seen."*
~ Ralph Waldo Emerson

DIVINE WILL is a belief in the Creator having a plan for humanity, and a desire to see this plan fulfilled. Divine will is allowing a desired outcome; personal will is imposing it. Energetically speaking, Divine will and personal will are opposites.

Western societies are embedded in personal will; Eastern societies practice Divine will. Personal will is a demonstration of fear; Divine will is a demonstration of faith. Personal will derives from the ego in the mind; Divine will derives from the opening of one's heart. The Creator desires us to allow Divine will to shape the world, manifesting an existence of 21st-century living.

Sleeping Souls tend to live in their minds. They tend to get ahead through imposing their personal wills. Because of their forceful actions, society tends to label them positively as achievers, go-getters, and leaders—validating and supporting their aggressive actions. For many, the thought of allowing Divine will to determine the outcome is ridiculous because it means surrendering control. Many Sleeping Souls need to control. And most times, their need to control is fueled by their fears, insecurities, and lack of faith. Some begin to seek.

Seekers generally have learned that Divine will directs the Divine order of life in the perfect Universe. They understand that Sleeping Souls imposing their personal wills disrupt the Divine flow of life on Earth. Seekers tend to examine how to get in sync with the patterns that allow their bodies to find their own rhythm without any resistance. In other words, they allow their bodies to become in sync with the Divine flow.

Awakened tend to believe that if the world's people simply moved their egos out of their minds through opening their hearts, choosing to listen through deep, reflective meditation, trusting what they heard, and allowing Divine will to unfold in their lives, we would instantly begin to shift into the new paradigm of 21st-century living, bringing about peace and harmony throughout the world. It is then that our rhythm and internal timing will be in sync with Mother Earth's heartbeat. They realize that most of the world's people are out of step with their body's natural rhythm. In other words, their minds, hearts, and spirits are out of balance. A global realignment is necessary to move into a harmonious flow with Nature and the Universe. Awakened also have come to realize that living in alignment with the spiritual realm, allowing Divine will to unfold their lives, requires a great deal of patience. . . .

DIVINE WILL

I surrender my personal will to Divine will.

_____

_____

_____

_____

_____

_____

Aspect #22

ESSENCE:

Living with Divine will requires patience.

CONTEXT

*"I have just three things to teach:
simplicity, patience, compassion.
These three are your greatest treasures."*

~ Lao Tzu

PATIENCE is the capacity to accept or tolerate delay, trouble, or suffering without getting angry or upset. Patience is a virtue, which is a behavior showing high moral standards. Patience requires trusting the Creator's pace. Along with forgiveness, patience is among our greatest attributes and one we need to strengthen.

In our modern world, patience has waned with the increasing speed of technology and emphasis on convenience. In other words, the speed of technology has made the world very impatient. The pace of our lives has continued to increase while our moral standards have decreased.

Our brutal media continually reinforce violence, sex, inequality, discrimination, materialism, and separateness, while doing next to nothing to promote goodness, simplicity, compassion, and well-being. Our brutal media have also superficially created a world living in denial of its own power, fueled by the corporatocracy. Our impatience and desire for immediate, short-term results, combined with our ignorance of long-term ramifications, has led us right to where we are today. Every thought, idea, behavior, and action has coalesced to create our world at the present time.

Sleeping Souls tend to be rather impatient. Many of their mindsets are fixated on immediate gratification. Too few give consideration to long-term outcomes. Many fill their days seeking what they want now despite future consequences. Many are impatient with their parents, classmates, co-workers, and friends. Impatience rules their lives. Some begin to seek.

Seekers tend to learn patience through aligning with Divine will, and realizing the Universe evolves infinitely and at a very slow pace. They learn the definition of Divine timing, which means that an event occurs in Divine order at the perfect time. Seekers learn that by living fully in the present time and enjoying life every day, they allow Divine will to unfold in their lives. Therefore, everything occurs in Divine timing, which requires patience.

Awakened tend to be patient and tolerant people. Their open-mindedness allows them to embrace the differences of others and enables them to relate to them regardless of where others are on their personal journeys. They tend to plant many seeds of opportunity and then allow each one to grow in Divine timing. They realize that allowing Divine will is *not* waiting for things to fall into their laps. Rather, action is required to manifest their dreams. And this action requires bravery. . . .

Patience

*I listen to the rhythm of my Soul.
And I trust the Creator's pace.*

_____

_____

_____

_____

_____

_____

Aspect #23

ESSENCE:

I am brave in all that I do.

"The bravest are surely those who have the clearest vision of what is before them, glory and danger alike, and yet notwithstanding, go out to meet it."
~ **Thucydides**

BRAVERY is courageous behavior or character. Bravery is necessary when carrying out our life's purpose, as there will undoubtedly be many challenges along the way.

Bravery provides us the strength to charge ahead, taking action in a positive way. The mindset of 21st-century living is that unless everybody does well, nobody does well. In our self-indulgent, modern world, this may be a hard pill to swallow, but it is a necessary cure for the state of planetary awareness today.

Sleeping Souls tend to use their bravery in destructive ways, including being callous, vindictive, and cunning. Many others are in need of bravery to break free from the shackles of limitation. For many Sleeping Souls, directing their bravery in productive ways will move them toward leading more joyous lives. Some begin to seek.

Seekers tend to realize that it takes courage to move to their next level of experience, displaying their bravery through focus, patience, and selflessness. They tend to disregard pettiness in their world, not through anger, but through living their truths with compassionate understanding for those who do not walk similar paths. Seekers tend to lead by example, using truth and courage.

Awakened tend always to be on alert to call upon their inner resources, having the willingness to take on the challenges of their present situations. They realize that their only barrier to advancement is their refusal to acknowledge the strength they possess within. Many realize the benefit of continuously addressing their challenges in the present, enabling them to be more self-confident in future situations. And they tend to be fearless in pursuit of their life's purpose, understanding their spiritual quest requires tremendous perseverance...

BRAVERY

I live my life with bravery.

Aspect #24

ESSENCE:

I persevere.

"Fall seven times, stand up eight."
~ **Japanese Proverb**

PERSEVERANCE is doing something despite difficulty and/or delay in achieving success. Perseverance is the strength we have to help carry us through difficult times. Perseverance is an intangible muscle, as the more we use it, the stronger it gets.

The illusion that money solves life's problems is just that, an illusion, meaning that wealthy people encounter challenges too. The point is, every single human needs perseverance to thrive in life.

Sleeping Souls tend to view problems as problems, adding more negativity to their lives. Many tend to hesitate, and not persevere, due to the fear of the unknown. Many persevere in areas that may not serve them well, such as dwelling on the negative, constantly complaining, gossiping about others, and/or being obsessed about making money at the expense of ignoring their families, friends, and Nature. Some begin to seek.

Seekers tend to view problems as challenges, placing what otherwise could be viewed as a negative in a positive context. They generally know that they are here for a certain purpose and therefore cannot stop moving toward their goals. Their inner knowing fuels their perseverance, and they have come to realize that a secret ingredient to success is to never quit so long as they remain inspired.

Awakened tend to persevere with grace and ease. This is due to being in alignment with their mind, body, spirit, and Soul, and in this way naturally attracting the resources required to manifest their true heart's desires and fulfill their life's purpose. They tend to avoid establishing preconceived timetables for when things will happen. Rather, they persevere through inspired action, aligning with the Divine flow, while allowing the events in their lives to occur according to Divine timing. And they have come to learn that the best way to persevere is through having a high degree of fortitude. . . .

PERSEVERANCE

*I will continue to persevere on my journey
until I manifest my true heart's desires
and fulfill my life's purpose.*

_____

_____

_____

_____

_____

Aspect #25

ESSENCE:

I have the strength to endure immense adversity with grace and ease.

CONTEXT

"Fortitude refers to the type of courage that permits one to endure tremendous pain with tremendous patience and calm."
~ Billy Mills

FORTITUDE is having courage in pain and/or adversity. We all experience challenges; we can face them with stress and drama, or we can learn to face them with patience and calmness. Like perseverance, fortitude is an intangible muscle; the more we use it, the stronger it gets.

A key attribute of fortitude is having clear intent. When we are clear with our intentions, we are able to flow with inspired action.

Sleeping Souls are generally not connected to their life's purpose. Therefore, many are not clear on their intent. Many believe that simply living is their intent, and therefore, life is lacking in meaning, leaving them unfulfilled. Many will talk about their intentions, whatever they may be, yet lack the strength to follow through—fortitude. Many will avoid their intent if it means dealing with struggles, challenges, or uncertainty. Sleeping Souls will generally look back on life with thoughts of would've, should've, could've. Some begin to seek.

Seekers tend to learn that having clear intent is important to remain focused. Many tend to realize that when they want to go in 10 directions at once, they need to go within for reflective meditation to regain clarity. The Seekers who have already discovered their life's purpose realize that fulfilling it will definitely require fortitude.

Awakened tend to live with conviction, remaining clear, decisive, and focused. They realize that all of creation has a separate intent and goal, whereby each person's specific purpose feeds the whole. They realize that life is challenging and therefore accept that they will need fortitude to carry out their vision. And even with all the challenges life poses, a large part of their centeredness is grounded in gratitude. . . .

FORTITUDE

*I am strong and capable.
And I live my life with grace and ease.*

Aspect #26

ESSENCE:

I am grateful for my life and for who I am.

CONTEXT

"He is a wise man who does not grieve for the things which he has not, but rejoices for those which he has."
~ **Epictetus**

GRATITUDE is the quality of being thankful, the readiness to show appreciation for and to return kindness. Gratitude includes celebrating life and acknowledging the beauty and potential of one's Self. Gratitude provides the basis for true abundance.

Many of us take our health for granted until we get sick. Many of us take family and friends for granted until someone close to us dies. Many of us dread going to school until after we graduate. Gratitude is generally realized after the fact, reflecting on a past time. Our world is plagued with a lack of gratitude in the present time.

Sleeping Souls tend to be so caught up in their drama-filled lives that gratitude is reserved for Thanksgiving dinner and religious holidays. Many never take the time to count their blessings—family, friends, food, health, shelter, love, fingers, toes, and senses. Many have difficulty expressing their true feelings of gratitude, because they are living in their minds. Many are extremely materialistic, focusing on what they don't have. The more selfish one tends to be, the less gratitude they tend to have in their lives. Some begin to seek.

Seekers tend to see the beauty of the world around them. Some will discover their renewed connection with Nature. They will make watching the sunset a part of their day and admiring the full moon a part of their month. Some will discover their renewed connection with family and other personal relationships. They will let other people know how much they appreciate them. Their gratefulness expands.

Awakened tend to count their blessings every day. Gratitude is at the core of their existence. As they go through their day, they tend to acknowledge the gratefulness they are experiencing: being grateful for waking up in the morning, being grateful when they buy groceries, being grateful when they get to spend time with family and/or friends, being grateful when they secure a new client. Awakened realize that gratitude is the ultimate state of existence for receiving, gracefully attracting into their lives experiences they desire. And through expanding their gratefulness, they tend to become very humble. . . .

GRATITUDE

*I am at peace with myself
and grateful in every area of my life.*

_____

_____

_____

_____

_____

_____

Aspect #27

ESSENCE:

**I remain humble in my success,
as I am simply fulfilling my life's purpose.**

*"Humility does not mean thinking less of yourself
than of other people, nor does it mean
having a low opinion of your own gifts.
It means freedom from thinking about yourself at all."*
~ **William Temple**

HUMILITY is a modest view of one's own importance—humbleness. Humility comes from having an open heart. Humility enables centeredness and humbleness to coincide with success in life.

Sleeping Souls have a tendency to adopt arrogance when they are successful in life, as their egos are in their minds, which means their hearts are closed. They tend to compare themselves to others through a lens of prestige, power, money, and control. Generally speaking, for Sleeping Souls, success breeds arrogance. Some begin to seek.

Seekers have a tendency to adopt humility when they are successful in life, as their hearts are opening. They tend to learn that they must become humble as they drop their disbelief and cynical ways. They realize that the wonder of life is always alive in those who replace their fears with faith.

ESSENCE

Awakened tend to be humble, living their lives with an open heart. For many, they haven't always been this way. Rather, they've acquired wisdom through enduring extremely difficult times. As a result, they come out of those times a different person. Through wisdom, they have learned gratefulness. Through gratefulness, they have learned humbleness. And, through humbleness, they have learned simplicity. . . .

HUMILITY

I am humble.

Aspect #28

ESSENCE:

I live a simple life.

CONTEXT

"Simplicity is the ultimate sophistication."
~ **Leonardo da Vinci**

SIMPLICITY is the quality or condition of being easy to understand or do. Simplicity captures the ESSENCE of 21st-century living: "Less is more. Keep it simple, stupid."

Mahatma Gandhi wisely stated, "There is enough for everybody's need, but not enough for anybody's greed." Abandonment of our materialistic mindsets is what's called for at this time. Become practical. Contemplate every purchasing decision. Take on no more debt, ever. Ensure that your thoughts, decisions, and behaviors align with the health and well-being of Mother Earth and ourselves. Reconnect with Nature. Reconnect with family and friends. Live in the present time. And simplify, simplify, simplify.

Sleeping Souls tend to feed right into the corporate marketing tactics that exploit the seven deadly sins—wrath, greed, sloth, pride, lust, envy, and gluttony—because that is what sells. Violent movies, sexy advertisements, luxury cars, extravagant jewelry, designer handbags, and a host of other products all feed into the materialistic, self-indulgent wants of society. Many Sleeping Souls acquire so much stuff that their lives are very cluttered. A cluttered house is a cluttered mind. Some come to realize that all their stuff is rather empty. And when this occurs, some begin to seek.

Seekers tend to no longer want clutter in their lives. Some might imagine that each possession they own has a golden cord attached to it that is connected to the heavens above. These cords surround them, so the more cords they have, the more clutter they have, and the more constricted their lives become. What becomes paramount in many Seekers' lives is freedom—freedom to move around, freedom to have balance in life, freedom from debt. They tend to become very selective of their possessions, choosing increased freedom instead. With newfound freedom, they rediscover joy, happiness, and companionship.

Awakened tend to live simply, enjoying the freedom of their lives. With their de-emphasis on materialistic pursuits, time and energy opens up to nurture other aspects of life such as relationships, physical activities, personal spiritual practice, hobbies, and reading. Many discover companionship through collaboration. . . .

SIMPLICITY

I live a simple life with very little drama.

Aspect #29

ESSENCE:

I achieve greater success by collaborating with others.

*"Teamwork divides the task
and amplifies the success."*
~ **Author Unknown**

COLLABORATION is the action of working with someone to produce or create something. Collaboration springs from an open heart and is an integral part of 21st-century living.

Separateness, competition, power, greed, and sloth have led to our global economic recession. What will change this economy is the banding together of like-hearted entrepreneurs and consumers who collectively collaborate; and through behavioral economics, create new markets that support 21st-century living.

Sleeping Souls tend to have an every-man-for-himself mindset. The concept of replacing competition with collaboration is foreign to many of them, because they live in their minds. The separation of age, gender, races, religions, corporate cultures, political parties, communities, states, and countries all stem from fear-based, mind-centered egos, which lack the mentality of collaboration. Many Sleeping Souls compete in almost everything they do. Some thrive, while others get exhausted from competing all of the time. Some begin to seek.

Seekers generally become adept at sharing their abilities, resources, and experiences. However, they choose consciously and carefully to spend their energy in ways that are productive, avoiding relationships that are high in drama or energy draining. Many reevaluate those they have chosen as friends and begin to establish connections with new acquaintances, ones who tend to be fellow Seekers or Awakened because of their collaborative nature, openness, and broadened perspective on life. They tend to realize quickly that their drama-filled lives are a part of their past. They are stepping into a new life of sharing, kindness, compassion, and a host of other positive attributes.

Awakened collaborate. Most tend to realize that "no man is an island," as we all depend upon each other, influenced by Nature and the Universe. Collaboration is an integral part of 21st-century living. Because Awakened are open hearted, they are not arrogant or selfish, and therefore they do not ignore the needs of the next seven generations. They know that remaining dependent upon shrinking finite resources—for example, oil, gas, coal, and clean water—means destroying the Earth and ourselves. Together we must *be* the difference by using available innovations including solar, wind, and geothermal power. And through the expansion of their awareness, many Awakened have successfully learned to utilize the positive vibrational frequencies of their mind, body, and spirit. . . .

COLLABORATION

*I work in collaboration with others
to help fuel our collective success.*

Aspect #30

ESSENCE:

Our minds receive and emit energy.

*"All action results from thought,
so it is thoughts that matter."*
~ Sai Baba

MIND ENERGY is powerful. Our minds constantly receive and emit energy. As it relates to the mind, energy is the strength and vitality required for sustained mental activity. When our minds are cluttered with drama, we block our creativity, limiting solutions to our challenges.

Like attracts like. If your mindset is fixated on fear, doubt, worries, drama, insecurity, and a host of other limiting thoughts, then your life will be negative and full of struggle. If your mindset is thriving with thoughts of prosperity, abundance, gratitude, respect, joy, happiness, and love, then your life will be positive and move in the Divine flow.

A misalignment between our conscious and subconscious minds sends mixed signals, or energetic vibrations, out into the Universe. By being unclear about our desires and purpose, we set ourselves up for failures. By being clear about our desires and purpose, we can manifest our lives by design instead of by default. The true success of living a vibrant and healthy lifestyle is contingent upon having the right mindset to do so. Our thoughts dictate our lives.

Sleeping Souls generally have a subconscious mindset that is negative and/or cluttered with limiting beliefs. It's not their fault; rather, it's a result of being born and raised in the old paradigm. Many tend not to realize that their conscious mind is protecting their subconscious mind from change. The conscious mind is formed through past experiences and is resistant to change. And, since Sleeping Souls' present-day existence is a culmination of past decisions, the conscious mind will protect them by keeping things as they are, because with change comes uncertainty. The irony is that the conscious mind will hold people captive to their current circumstances even if these are not what they desire. Some begin to seek.

Seekers tend to learn the connection between their thoughts, emotions, decisions, and actions. They realize the collection of all these forms their lives. Many are seeking ways to reprogram their subconscious minds, replacing negative, limiting beliefs with a new mindset of positive, infinite beliefs.

Awakened tend to have masterfully reprogrammed their subconscious minds with these positive, infinite beliefs, elevating their mind's energetic vibration and strengthening their connection with the higher dimensions. Many Awakened realize the importance of having not only clear mind energy, but also strong body energy. . . .

MIND ENERGY

My mind is filled with positive thoughts.

_____

_____

_____

_____

_____

_____

Aspect #31

ESSENCE:

Our bodies receive and emit energy.

CONTEXT

*"Worthless people live only to eat and drink;
people of worth eat and drink only to live."*
~ Socrates

BODY ENERGY reflects the physical condition of our bodies. Our bodies are the temples for our Souls, so the greater care we have for our temples, the more body energy we can generate. The key to full aliveness is having a healthy body.

Body energy is correlated to the physical condition of the temple it occupies. According to the Census Bureau, approximately 14% of people worldwide are overweight and 5% are considered obese. Speaking only for the United States, about 60% to 65% are overweight and about 30% are obese. It's time we got into shape, which, for some, requires temperance.

But body energy is not limited to physical activity such as walking, running, and jumping. Every cell, molecule, and atom carries knowledge and wisdom. Our bodies operate as our very own antennae: We can sense when we are or are not safe, we can sense when someone is staring at us, and we can sense the energetic vibrations of others, enabling us to tell instantly if someone is in a good or bad mood without them uttering a word.

Sleeping Souls tend not to have a strong awareness of their body energies beyond physical activity. They tend not to explore the deeper senses of body energies, ignoring gut instincts and intuitive impulses. Many regret their actions in hindsight, wishing they had followed their gut instincts and intuition. Yet, when the opportunity arises again, they will repeat the same old pattern. This may be due to their low faith and trust in the intangible aspects of life, including their higher Selves. Some begin to seek.

Seekers tend to feel their way through challenges, utilizing their body energies and intuition to guide them. Their faith in the intangible and themselves continues to grow. They tend to treat their bodies as temples, realizing the correlation between physical condition and the level of energy they can hold and emit. Nutrition becomes paramount. Many begin to work out to lose body fat and build muscle. They tend to eat organic foods, paying attention to where their food comes from.

Awakened generally feel the joy of having a physical—and spiritual—body. Many are physically fit, honoring the body's role and its needs. They understand the correlation between a strong body and a clear mind. Many observe a daily practice that includes physical exercise, nutritional eating, and spiritual meditation. And many Awakened realize that a keen awareness of the body enables them to find the power place within, facilitating access to their spirit energy. . . .

*The stronger I make my body,
the more energy I can hold and emit.*

_____

_____

_____

_____

_____

_____

Aspect #32

ESSENCE:

My spirit is energy.

CONTEXT

"We can easily forgive a child who is afraid of the dark; the real tragedy of life is when men are afraid of the light."

~ Plato

SPIRIT ENERGY is infinite energy. A strong body with a positive mindset and an open heart connects us to this powerful and limitless energy. Perseverance and fortitude draw from spirit energy. Spirit energy is our life-energy force, which returns to the pool of life energy upon our passing.

Sleeping Souls tend to survive, consciously, only on mental and body energies, without realizing their heart and spirit energy are also at work. Subconsciously, of course, they are still operating as threefold beings comprising mind, body, and spirit; even while their Souls sleep, spirit energy fuels their lives. Many Sleeping Souls are tired of the struggle, the daily grind, working so hard to make ends meet, only to come home, ignore their families, and crash on the couch in front of the television. Some Sleeping Souls realize that there must be more to life. Some begin to seek.

Seekers tend to make dramatic changes in their lives, and quickly. For starters, they stop watching television and reading the newspaper. They recognize that both are filled with fear, doubt, worries, drama, insecurity, and a host of other low-vibrating frequencies that they no longer desire in their lives. Many will begin walking or jogging. Many will begin a daily spiritual practice such as yoga, meditation, or journaling. Many will start hiking in the woods, reconnecting with Nature. Many will give up fast foods, stop drinking soda, and begin to drink a lot of water. In hindsight, they tend to realize that what was holding them captive in their Sleeping Souls' lifestyle was their fear of change. Most every Seeker feels blessed for encountering the gauntlet of challenges required for change, thus building a deeper connection with their Spirit through Self-love. Their Souls begin to awaken.

Awakened realize they are not just threefold beings but fourfold ones comprising mind, body, spirit, and Soul. Their sleeping Souls have awakened by living through the opening of their hearts. They tend to realize that their Souls are their very being. Their spirits, moreover, are their life energy force, and they tend to connect deeply with that spirit energy. They understand the connections among all four dimensions of being, realizing the importance of balance in their lives. And they have successfully released negative emotions from their past. They tend not to dwell too much on the future, because they have learned the importance of living fully in present time. . . .

SPIRIT ENERGY

I realize who I am: mind, body, spirit, and Soul.

_____

_____

_____

_____

_____

_____

Aspect #33

ESSENCE:

The only time is present time.

CONTEXT

"Do not dwell in the past, do not dream of the future, concentrate the mind on the present moment."
~ Buddha

PRESENT TIME is occurring now. Life on Earth only exists in present time. Humans fabricated time. Before we inhabited the Earth, life simply existed in a state of being.

In other words, time doesn't really exist. It is an illusion, purely a human mechanism for managing our lives. Outside the human framework, all other organisms live in the now, as there is no yesterday or tomorrow in their consciousness. Of course, other organisms learn things and use that knowledge at a later date, but don't confuse this with having a framework of time.

In the 1902 book *Sun Dials and Roses of Yesterday* by Alice Morse Earle, she noted the wisdom, "Yesterday is history. Tomorrow is a mystery. Today is a gift. That's why it is called the present." Within the human mechanism known as time, it is important that we place great emphasis on being fully present.

Sleeping Souls generally spend very little time being present. Their minds tend to race, dwelling on past memories or future illusions. Those who are dwelling on past time most likely view themselves as victims. Those that are dwelling on future time most likely are dreamers living an illusion. Many miss the beauty of Nature and human interactions because they spend very little time being present. Some begin to seek.

Seekers tend to learn the importance of being fully present. As they traverse to the new paradigm of 21st-century living, their perspective expands, realizing the power of now. They release the old belief of working hard today in order to enjoy tomorrow. They tend to simply enjoy living in the present, as they choose to work and play with ease.

Awakened have healed past wounds, embracing an unknown future while living in present time. They are grateful for the blessing of simply being alive. They tend to realize that their greatest focus, strength, and creativity occur in present time. And through being fully present and heart centered, they tend to experience unlimited vision. . . .

*I live fully in the present and
am open to all possibilities.*

Aspect #34

ESSENCE:

**If I have all the answers,
then my vision is too small.**

"Nothing is impossible, the word itself says 'I'm possible.'"
~ **Audrey Hepburn**

VISION is the ability to think about or plan the future with imagination and wisdom. Visionaries are open to the infinite, having an uncanny ability to see opportunity amid chaos.

Successfully manifesting our mind's vision into three-dimensional form requires leveraging the mind, body, and spirit energies. Every thought of every person reflects the collective consciousness of our society. Every thought, light and dark, is already created as a potential outcome in the higher dimensions. Based on our own personal energetic vibration, we are choosing which potential outcomes we are attracting into our lives. To varying degrees, all of us are alchemists—possessing a seemingly magical process of transformation and manifestation.

Sleeping Souls tend to believe that their success is driven by their determination, fueled by their egos in their minds. Their never-quit attitude certainly helps them to achieve. However, what many Sleeping Souls fail to realize is that no matter how successful they become, unless they tap into their inner knowing and leverage their innate energies, they will never fully maximize their potential. Many Sleeping Souls don't believe that dreams come true. Hence, they are incapable of bringing their visions to life. Others have their minds so cluttered with negative thoughts that there's no room for their visions to even enter. Some only experience vision or dreams when their conscious minds have quieted during sleep. Some desire to make their dreams come true. Some begin to seek.

Seekers generally learn the power of manifesting their dreams. They tend to learn how to align their energies to choose the potential outcomes they attract into their lives. Many find life boring unless they are building their dreams. As they envision the future, many are willing to ask for the resources to bring their dreams to life, and they are willing to receive these resources as they appear in Divine timing. They generally learn that if they have all the answers, then their vision is too small—always leaving room for the spirit realm to assist.

Awakened dream *big*. They tend to always have their eyes open, noticing the world around them—the ocean, the mountains, the life force in every living thing. They see everything and every person as their teachers. They see the precious gift and beauty of life. They live their dreams through building their visions with creativity and passion. And, when building their visions, they do so with focus. . . .

VISION

*With vision, everything is possible
and everything is solvable.*

Aspect #35

ESSENCE:

My focus inspires me.

CONTEXT

*"Focus on the journey, not the destination.
Joy is found not in finishing an activity but in doing it."*
~ Greg Anderson

FOCUS is an act of concentrating interest or activity on something. When manifesting a vision, intense focus is necessary to create the vision in three-dimensional form.

Focus enables us to continue to take the necessary steps in present time to create what we have in mind. Perseverance and patience, most times, accompany focus in our efforts to create. Remaining focused during challenging and stressful times is an important element for each of us to learn.

Sleeping Souls tend to have a difficult time focusing, due to the stress, worry, and doubt that plague their lives. Many have "pockets of focus," which vary based on their mood. They have difficulty sustaining focus over the long term, short-circuiting their ability to achieve their goals. Many get frustrated and quit. Some begin to seek.

Seekers tend to learn rather quickly the importance of focus. Their lives are becoming much more about living in present time, not dwelling on past memories or future illusions. As a result, their focus is in a constant state of present creation. Many tend to create visions of the future while being fully aware of the present-day focus necessary to create these visions into reality.

Awakened tend to be 21st-century alchemists. Historically speaking, alchemists could turn iron into gold; a 21st-century alchemist can turn a thought and vision into anything they desire. Most are familiar with the *Law of Attraction*, which requires one to be energetically vibrating at an extremely high frequency while maintaining a high sense of focus on creation. Many concentrate all their focus upon the work at hand, refusing to have their focus dissipate when life isn't going their way. And they tend to be inspired through being intensely focused in present time, successfully manifesting their visions while being in a natural state of profound contemplation. . . .

*My focus inspires me
to manifest my vision into reality.*

_____

_____

_____

_____

_____

_____

Aspect #36

ESSENCE:

I think before I act.

"We are what we think. All that we are arises with our thoughts. . . . Speak or act with an impure mind, and trouble will follow you. . . . Speak or act with a pure mind, and happiness will follow you."
~ The Dhammapada

CONTEMPLATION is the action of looking thoughtfully at something for a long time—deep reflective thought. We are what we think, we are what we eat, and we are who we believe we are. Hence, contemplation regarding our mind, body, and spirit is crucial.

Contemplation enables us to attain greater levels of understanding before we act. Many of our regrets stem from acting first, thinking second. Oftentimes we find it difficult to correct our past actions: apologizing for words spoken, but not meant, spending time in our own personal prison pondering how we could have conducted ourselves differently, regretting being irresponsible during challenging times. Contemplation is an intangible muscle, like forgiveness and fortitude; the more we use it, the stronger it becomes.

Sleeping Souls tend to be out of balance. When they are not centered, they tend to make poor choices that do not serve them well; contemplation is often a missing component. Many Sleeping Souls know what they are doing is not serving them, yet they continue to do it anyway. Perhaps they are faced with the fear of not fitting in. Perhaps they lack the bravery to stand on their own two feet. Many Sleeping Souls would benefit by facing their fears, acquiring bravery through experience, and contemplating decisions so as to positively influence their actions. Many Sleeping Souls want to make better choices. Some begin to seek.

Seekers tend to contemplate through connecting with Nature and their inner knowing. When their minds are cluttered, going for a walk in the woods or in a city green space tends to clear out the cobwebs. Many begin to learn about the powerful energies that reside in Nature. Many Seekers tend to carry a special stone to help continually ground them. Many will hold this stone in their hand when contemplating a decision, quieting any negative mind chatter, and creating space for new solutions to appear.

Awakened tend to access their inner knowing through contemplation. They use their knowledge and wisdom to make choices that serve them well. Awakened tend to not be in a hurry, instead taking the time to contemplate matters. In the contemplation process, many have learned to observe everything through a lens of acceptance. . . .

CONTEMPLATION

*I contemplate my thoughts before I act,
to choose the right decisions for my life.*

Aspect #37

ESSENCE:

I accept that we are aspects of a perfect Universe.

"Be curious, not judgmental."
~ Walt Whitman

ACCEPTANCE is avoiding moral judgments. We each have our own unique story, and respecting this uniqueness is a key to living life with nonjudgment.

Anything or anyone that judges, separates, or controls is old paradigm. Being judgmental fuels racial discrimination, gender disparities, religious differences, and separatism. Traversing from being judgmental to nonjudgmental begins with acceptance. Acceptance that, according to neuroscience, we are 99.99% the same, as our human differences represent one-100th of 1%. Acceptance that we are connected with Nature, including the birds, trees, mountains, oceans, rocks, and streams. Acceptance that we are an aspect of the Universe and therefore an aspect of the infinite. Acceptance of our differences, acceptance of our similarities.

Sleeping Souls tend to be judgmental. They view the world through a lens of extremely low awareness and an extremely narrow perspective. They tend to spend their time convincing others why they are right, while judging people and circumstances through their finite conscious minds. Sleeping Souls tend to fear others who look differently, speak differently, and dress differently. Their judgment tends to hold them in fear of others, causing them to miss out on the opportunity to explore aspects of the Universe they've yet to discover. Some begin to seek.

Seekers tend to learn to accept themselves as they ascend out of their internal dramas. They no longer judge the Sleeping Souls as they did when they, too, were Sleeping Souls. They generally adopt a new level of character and self-sufficiency, and could care less when Sleeping Souls judge them. Seekers generally learn to handle life with ease, taking responsibility for themselves and their actions.

Awakened accept themselves with love and compassion. They respect each person's unique story and don't waste energy trying to convince others of their story. They tend to view diversity as a strength and equality as simply a way of life. They tend to be excellent observers of situations and people while refusing to attach to any associated judgmental energy. They simply observe to learn and contemplate. They realize that the energy associated with judging carries a low vibrational energy, whereas acceptance carries a high vibrational energy. They naturally gravitate to the high vibration. They tend to realize that in order to access the Divine flow of life, acceptance is a requirement, along with willingness. . . .

ACCEPTANCE

*I accept myself. I accept the infinite.
I accept I am infinite.*

Aspect #38

ESSENCE:

I willingly release judgments.

CONTEXT

"Don't worry about a thing, every little thing is gonna be alright."
~ **Bob Marley**

WILLINGNESS, in a spiritual context, is the practice of remaining open to and accepting all opportunities that serve our highest good. Nonresistance is free of judging, free of fixating on preconceived outcomes, and free of imposing our personal wills.

Nonresistance enables us to remain open beyond our current realm of conscious thinking. It means remaining open to the infinite, having faith and trust in our higher Selves to determine the best path to travel. Nonresistance means truly listening to others and observing our surroundings, as the spirit realm speaks to us through different people and through different situations that arise.

Sleeping Souls tend to live with a high degree of resistance. They tend to fixate on how they want something to be and then exert their personal wills to contort the situation to their liking. Many experience that big expectations lead to big disappointments. Sleeping Souls generally become burned out by trying so hard to execute what they have in mind. Control, manipulation, and coercion are part of their arsenal for getting things done.

Many are highly competitive and will simply outwork, outmaneuver, and outrank others in order to win at any cost. Some believe it's better to cheat and win in order to not lose. Many Sleeping Souls are sleep deprived, as their racing minds keep them up at night. Many want off the hamster wheel. Some begin to seek.

Seekers tend to traverse from doing to allowing, replacing personal will with Divine will. As their edginess from living in the old 20th-century paradigm softens, their need to make things look a certain way dissipates. Their listening skills tend to improve considerably. They begin to view situations from multiple perspectives, discovering the ways in which numerous outcomes can occur. Even so, they remain open to other possible outcomes, releasing resistance and choosing to listen to their hearts instead of their minds. Seekers begin to know that judgment is resistance.

Awakened tend to have trust, faith, and belief that as long as they live with willingness, allowing Divine will to determine the outcome, then their aspect of the Universal plan will naturally take care of itself. They realize that willingness comes from the heart, whereas resistance comes from the mind. They tend to establish their vision, align their energies, and allow the situation to unfold naturally. They remain open to change when new facts are presented. By living in nonresistance, they effectively align with the high energetic vibrations of abundance, including money. . . .

WILLINGNESS

I willingly accept abundance, without any resistance.

Aspect #39

ESSENCE:

Money is energy.

CONTEXT

"An investment in knowledge pays the best interest."
~ **Benjamin Franklin**

MONEY ENERGY has a wide bandwidth. Money is a medium of exchange; however, what most people don't realize is that money is energy. Building a positive, high energetic vibration and healthy relationship with money will naturally attract more money into our lives.

Sleeping Souls tend to have a poor relationship with money. For many, their minds are fixated on scarcity, constantly worrying about whether they will have enough. Because like attracts like, they get exactly what they don't want. Many are extremely financially successful but live in fear that they will lose it or someone will take it. Others believe that it's bad to be rich. Some are consistent underearners due to low self-worth, viewing life as a struggle. Some have a tough time remaining focused, jumping from one opportunity to the next, never realizing their full money-making capacities. Some begin to seek.

Seekers tend to discover for the first time that money is energy. If thoughts of scarcity, lack, or fear regarding money come to mind, they tend to take corrective action quickly to feel good, eliminating any negative thoughts from their existence. Because a significant part of their journey is about discovering the energetic vibrations of the mind, body, and spirit, their ability to align with the high vibration of money becomes rather natural.

Awakened tend to understand the utmost importance of building and maintaining a healthy relationship with money. They also tend to understand the importance of identifying their true heart's desires and emitting clear, high **energetic vibrational frequencies** to the Universe. They realize that a materialistic and greedy mindset has a low energetic vibration, whereas a simplistic and life-purpose mindset has a high energetic vibration. Many become financially successful, positioning themselves to help others who are less fortunate, demonstrating their high degree of compassion. . . .

Money is energy. Investing in myself always pays off.

_____

_____

_____

_____

_____

_____

Aspect #40

ESSENCE:

I give to give, not give to get.

*"If you want others to be happy, practice compassion.
If you want to be happy, practice compassion."*
~ Dalai Lama

COMPASSION is the sympathetic concern for the sufferings or misfortunes of others. If our hearts are closed, compassion cannot expand. As we love and care for one another, our compassion increases. The more open our hearts become, the more we feel concern and love for others.

Compassion is not limited to other people, as it includes ourselves. We need to nurture ourselves. Do we get enough sound sleep? Do we eat well? Do we exercise? Do we meditate? Do we listen to our bodies? Do we allow ourselves to feel emotions welling up inside of us? Do we allow ourselves to be authentic? Nurturing ourselves enables us to help nurture others.

Sleeping Souls tend to have a more self-centered nature than a compassionate one. Many that do nurture themselves tend to focus primarily on the physical aspects of their outer looks while not spending too much time within, connecting with their hearts, thereby becoming more compassionate. Some Sleeping Souls are philanthropists who own major companies that are decimating the Earth and her people. Generally, their compassionate gestures —donating large sums of money—are not authentic; many are simply feeding their egos while positioning themselves and their companies in a positive light in the public eye. Many Sleeping Souls are, however, truly compassionate people who find themselves in desperate situations, limiting their compassion for others by being solely focused on their own present-day lives. Some begin to seek.

Seekers tend to transition to heart-centered lives. As their hearts open they become more compassionate, feeling the elation of helping and caring for others. They tend to learn that compassion is not so much about giving from the wallet but about giving from the heart. Volunteering, listening, supporting, encouraging, loving, and coaching are all non-monetary gestures of compassion.

Awakened tend to give from their hearts and their wallets. They've learned the importance of giving without expecting anything in return. They give to give, not give to get. Their humbleness ensures them freedom from thinking of themselves. And, through their wisdom, they tend to understand the Universal law of giving and receiving. . . .

COMPASSION

I live my life with compassion for others and myself.

_____

_____

_____

_____

_____

Aspect #41

ESSENCE:

The best time to give is during the time of greatest need.

CONTEXT

"Love the giver more than the gift."
~ **Brigham Young**

GIVING & RECEIVING are a part of the Universal law that everything naturally moves in balance. In the highest sense, to give is to freely offer something valuable, whether tangible or intangible, to another. To receive is to accept what is being given, whether tangible or intangible, with gratitude and humility.

Ironically, based on the Universal law of balance, the best time to give is during the greatest time of need. In our infinite Universe, everything is connected and everything is balanced. If we are in a desperate situation, then giving to others will send pure energetic vibrations into the Universe, and through balance, the Universe will respond with pure energetic vibrations of receiving. Therefore, resources, financial and otherwise, will automatically start showing up in our lives.

Sleeping Souls tend to have a *take & get* mentality. Their days tend to be focused on getting what they want. Some are very successful at taking and getting but fail to realize that their out-of-balance karma will eventually catch up with them.

This is why many millionaires lose it all. Some Sleeping Souls become miserly because of their fear of not being able to sustain the cash flow needed to maintain their lives. Since their focus is self-centered, the thought of giving to others is uncommon. Some Sleeping Souls continually struggle with getting, so the thought of giving is nonexistent. Some begin to seek.

Seekers tend to learn that both giving and receiving have energetic vibrations, and like money energy, building a healthy relationship with them is fruitful. Many Seekers discover, through experiencing their own personal struggles, the joy that arises through the generosity of helping others. They tend to learn that the Universe will provide ample abundance for those with a giving nature.

Awakened tend to fully understand the Universal law of giving and receiving. They realize that the more they give, the more they receive, and they choose to do both in abundance. In other words, they give to give, not give to get, while knowing that despite expecting nothing in return, the Universe will automatically send them offerings in response—displaying a *give & receive* mentality. Awakened tend to be open to receiving without resistance, while getting true fulfillment by giving to others. And, with their eXpansive awareness and broadened perspective, they view the world we live in through a lens of equality. . . .

GIVING & RECEIVING

I am fulfilled by giving to others.

Aspect #42

ESSENCE:

We are all equal to one another.

*"The defect of equality is that
we desire it only with our superiors."*
~ Henry Becque

EQUALITY is the state of being equal, especially in status, rights, and opportunities. In the spiritual sense, equality is the idea that we are all aspects of the Divine, experiencing life at various levels of awareness, and nobody is superior or inferior to another. Equality erases separateness and fosters inclusiveness. And with inclusiveness comes acceptance.

An illusion of equality plagues this world. The word "humankind" refers to human beings considered collectively but is really an oxymoron—a contradiction of "human" and "kind" because since inception humans have not generally been kind to one another. A more fitting word to collectively describe humans would be "human-inequality." In civilization after civilization, wars and separateness have destroyed people's lives. One would think that by the 21st century we would have figured out how to live in peace and harmony with each other and ourselves. The reality is that we do, in fact, know what it takes to live in peace and harmony. And the solution is rather simple: Depart from the old paradigm of 20th-century living, and traverse to the new paradigm of 21st-century living. A foundational aspect of the new paradigm is belief in equality. This exit strategy requires bravery and fortitude.

Sleeping Souls tend to feed the inequality that exists in the world. Many live judgmental lives based on separateness, prejudice, and superiority. Most fail to realize that we are all made of the same atoms, connected to and drawing from the same Divine energy source, and we are all equal. Many Sleeping Souls are exhausted from living their judgmental lives. Some begin to seek.

Seekers tend to begin seeing images of themselves in other people through increased levels of awareness. They begin to eliminate the *"I"* while summoning the *"we,"* deepening their understanding of equality. They tend to recognize that all things are connected, and through acknowledging connectedness, a sense of equality emerges. They tend to learn that Nature is not here to serve us; rather, we are an aspect of Nature.

Awakened simply view everyone and everything as equals. Their view of the world, their perspective, is so broad that it is from outer space, where there are no divisions, boundaries, or limitations. They view the world as One global family. They realize that all parents want the best for their children. They know that we are all children of the Divine. They want the best for everybody. And they desire the world to become One family, living in unity. . . .

EQUALITY

I view everyone and everything as equals.

Aspect #43

ESSENCE:

Unity bonds our collective strength.

CONTEXT

"In union there is strength."
~ Aesop

UNITY is the state of being united or joined as a whole. Unity begins with one's Self and requires centeredness and balance. Unity begins with feeling at home with one's Self and evolves in harmony with all life. When the people of this world become centered and balanced, an awakened, unified global community will emerge.

Sleeping Souls tend to be imbalanced, often living in their minds, driven by fear and illusions of separateness. Their collective imbalance has kept the global community imbalanced. Sleeping Souls represent the greatest part of the challenge, yet they also are the greatest part of the solution. Some begin to seek.

Seekers tend to discover the wholeness of life. As they traverse to the new paradigm of 21st-century living, they are awakening to their potential. They tend to experience discomfort as they shed limiting beliefs and aspects of their old selves, similarly to a caterpillar. They understand that at the end of a caterpillar's life it believes life is over; yet, after enduring a period of uncertainty, the caterpillar morphs into a beautiful butterfly. Seekers tend to apply this analogy to their own journey toward becoming Awakened.

Awakened tend to realize that an expansion of awareness, traversing from the old paradigm to the new paradigm, needs to occur in order for unity to progress. This progression does not require cooperation from 51% of the world's population to establish a major shift. Rather, the actual number is closer to a mere 10%! Arlene Rose Curley explains in her book, *Completing the Seven*, what is known as the Hundredth Monkey Effect:

> Although the exact number may vary, this Hundredth Monkey Phenomenon means that when only a limited number of people know of a new way, it may remain conscious property of these people. But there is a point at which if only one more person tunes into a new awareness, the field is strengthened so that this awareness is picked up by almost everyone! . . . When enough people have gone through their personal version of the shift to the new consciousness, then a critical mass will form, and suddenly everyone will become aware of the New Reality and its heart-centered values. That is the day when heart-centered values will become the focus of everyday thinking for the vast majority of people. That is the day when humanity will begin to look back on what has changed and realize that a massive shift has occurred.

Awakened know this will be so, and the world will be full of love. . . .

UNITY

*I am an aspect of the togetherness
that bonds our unified community.*

Aspect #44

ESSENCE:

Love is the ultimate ESSENCE of life.

CONTEXT

"You come to love not by finding the perfect person, but by seeing an imperfect person perfectly."

~ Sam Keen

LOVE is an intense feeling of deep affection. Love is being connected. Love is being balanced. Love is being heart-centered. Love is Self-love. Love is forgiving. Love is being authentic. Love is being compassionate. Love is being truthful. Love is being trustworthy. Love is faith in aliveness. Love is having belief. Love is being patient. Love is being grateful. Love is being humble. Love is being collaborative. Love is living in present time. Love is contemplation. Love is being nonjudgmental. Love is being nonresistant. Love is having compassion. Love is giving. Love is receiving. Love is equality. Love is unity. Love is so much more, because love is infinite.

Sleeping Souls tend to struggle with love. Many live in their minds with closed hearts. Their fear, doubt, worries, drama, and insecurity tend to pose major barriers to the opening of their hearts. Many think they understand love, yet they have not felt true love in their hearts. Many desire to love and be loved, though. As the world continues to traverse to the new paradigm, many will begin to seek.

Seekers tend to be transitioning to a heart-centered life. As their hearts open, room for love, joy, and happiness expands. They tend to become grateful for the blessing of living life and really enjoy sharing their love with others.

Awakened tend to realize that all space is sacred space; within it, everyone and everything deserves to be loved and respected. They realize that our children are our tomorrows; accordingly, they have the right to live in safety, harmony, and affection with a healthy Mother Earth. Awakened tend to view adults as teachers, endowed with the mission of teaching 21st-century living to our children, as role models for them and the next seven generations. Through observing the behavior of adults, our children learn to love and respect themselves, each other, and Mother Earth!

LOVE

*I send thoughts of love,
and love returns in overflowing measure.*

*"When one realises one is asleep,
at that moment one is already half-awake."*
~ **P.D. Ouspensky**

AT THE BEGINNING of your journey, you were encouraged to establish a baseline measure of your current level of awakening by taking the **ESSENCE Assessment (EA44)**. It's now time to take the **EA44** again to determine your current level of awakening.

Take the **EA44** again now:
21stCenturyParadigm.com/ESSENCE-Assessment/

Once you have completed this assessment, compare the results to your **Round One Results** to calculate your progress in awakening your Soul.

Calculating My Awakening

1. Record **Total Points** and **Awakening %** on the **Round Two Results** line in the table below.

2. Refer to page 6 to retrieve **Round One Results**, and record them in the table below.

ESSENCE

3. Subtract **Round One Results** from the **Round Two Results**, calculating the **Awakening Variance**.

Round of Results	Total Points (Out of 220)	Awakening % (Out of 100%)
Round Two Results		%
Round One Results		%
Awakening Variance		%

A positive Awakening Variance percentage reflects the awakening of your sleeping Soul. A negative Awakening Variance percentage reflects an increasing level of resistance, closing your Soul even more. In either instance, there is always more work to do in the never-ending unfolding of ourselves.

In addition, we suggest you read ESSENCE multiple times, as it as rather difficult to fully integrate the amount of wisdom contained in the 44 Aspects after reading it just once. Some people choose to review one of the Aspects each day so they may consistently look more deeply into themselves.

Another strategy to is establish a daily practice of asking your Soul:

What do I need to see and learn about myself today?

Then open the book to the Aspect to which you are intuitively guided.

You can also compare your results to the diagram on our Web site, tracking your journey to a state of awakening. 21stCenturyParadigm.com/Awakening/

Lastly, the following table enables you to monitor your level of awakening over the long term.

Round of Results	Total Points (Out of 220)	Awakening % (Out of 100%)
Round One Results		%
Round Two Results		%
Round Three Results		%
Round Four Results		%
Round Five Results		%
Round Six Results		%
Round Seven Results		%
Round Eight Results		%
Round Nine Results		%
Round Ten Results		%

"There are no easy answers, but there are simple answers. We must have the courage to do what we know is morally right."
~ Ronald Reagan

DECISION TIME is now, in this present moment. We've captured the ESSENCE of 44 wonderful Aspects describing the new paradigm of 21st-century living, and the decision to change your story is now within your power. Our collective decisions, which reflect our collective consciousness, will determine the destiny of future generations living on Mother Earth.

As the Y-graphic on page 280 depicts, we realize, in hindsight, that many countries around the world have experienced various degrees of growth, prosperity, and abundance since the 1940s, especially the United States. However, the karma of overspending, overindulging, corruption, greed, power, and control finally caught up to us, leading to a global recession in 2008.

During this global recession, many of us experienced great turmoil, uncertainty, worry, doubt, and overall fear. It was also then that the U.S. government financially salvaged the banking system, the automobile industry, and the financial services and insurance industries, among others. It was a time of massive corruption, vastly eroding our

ESSENCE

middle class while fueling the prosperity of the richest 1%.

Then, according to Carl Johan Calleman—one of the world's foremost experts on the Mayan calendar—May 24th, 2017 occurred, which may be regarded as the beginning of a sustained effort to facilitate people in creating resonance. This day reflects a fork in the road, signifying that the chaos in the world has come to a point where it becomes necessary to create resonance on a larger collective scale with the wave that generates enlightened unity consciousness.

Decision Time

In other words, an eXpansive pathway has emerged, inspiring us to choose a new story filled with love, joy, freedom, abundance, and peace. Decision time is now. Which path are you taking?

Sleeping Souls tend to naively believe the Mayan calendar is a hoax. Through their limited perspective, they're unable to see and experience the shift in collective consciousness that continues to grow today. As a result, most Sleeping Souls continue to plod along the constrictive path, believing it will lead them back to the prosperous times of yesteryear. Through their limited perspective, they're unable to see the larger picture. Many continue to believe that we are separate from Nature and each other. Many remain dependent on people outside of themselves—politicians, corporate executives, lawyers, teachers, accountants, and doctors—thinking that others will somehow save them. Many now realize this isn't true. Even while experiencing the chaos, most people remain unchanged. They complain about wanting a new life, yet do very little seeking in order to create one. Most fail to realize that they're manifesting what they don't want—a life of drama and scarcity. And, since their behaviors haven't changed much, they continue to deplete and destroy Mother Earth through their actions. Most fail to realize that they are contributing to the potential outcome of *Civilization Dies* (as seen on the Y-graphic, page 280). Some begin to seek.

Seekers have the bravery to seek a new way of life. Consciously or subconsciously, they decide to take the eXpansive path. They took a journey inside themselves, questioning their beliefs and recognizing their limitations, while realizing that creating a new life in the 21st century involves taking personal accountability for their thoughts, behaviors, and actions. Many seek ways to reprogram their subconscious minds, instill a new belief system, and transition their lives to 21st-century living. This new belief system includes the awareness that we are an infinite aspect of the Universe, we are all connected as One, and we are a reflection of Nature because we are Nature itself. Therefore, how we treat Mother Earth is a reflection of how we treat ourselves. Many Seekers also break free from the shackles of relying on other people to fix their problems, while accepting the responsibility of manifesting the lives they desire. They've learned that like energy attracts like energy, so reprogramming their minds to emit positive energetic vibrations by having positive feelings and thoughts, has significantly helped them transition their consciousness. Most every Seeker comes to realize that the answers they're seeking reside within themselves. They learn to unleash their power from within, changing their intentions, behaviors and actions to reflect 21st-century living.

Awakened tend to already be living a 21st-century life. Most have awakened to a state of peacefulness, harmony, and balance, living in simplicity. Most Awakened support those who are seeking while continuing themselves to seek. They know the Universe is infinite and therefore they, and learning, are infinite too. Awakened have been successful in traversing to the new paradigm of 21st-century living.

PERSONAL VISION

SINCE YOU'VE COMPLETED reading the 44 Aspects of the ESSENCE, along with discovering that most of the world's population is living on the constrictive path, the question to consider is:

Are you inspired to create a new personal vision, traversing to a new life in the 21st century?

If yes, then we suggest that you create this vision utilizing your personal notes from the *Reflections* section of each Aspect.

In addition, we suggest you review the proceeding table summarizing each Aspect, comparing the old paradigm of 20th-century living to the new paradigm of 21st-century living.

Then create your new personal vision by journaling the vision for your new life, which includes the changes you commit to make utilizing each of the 44 Aspects.

Once you agree and choose to align with this new vision, your inspiration awakens, unleashing your power from within, manifesting this new personal vision into three-dimensional reality. Read your vision daily, deeply feeling and attracting it into your life as if it has already happened.

ESSENCE

ESSENCE Aspect	Old-Paradigm, 20th-Century Living	New-Paradigm, 21st-Century Living
Aspect #1: Self-Awareness	Constrictive Awareness, Narrow Perspective	eXpansive Awareness, Infinite Perspective
Aspect #2: Infinite Being	Finite Beliefs	Infinite Beliefs
Aspect #3: Connectedness	We-Are-Separate Mindset	We-Are-One Mindset
Aspect #4: Balance	Constrictive Understanding of the Balanced Universe	eXpansive Understanding of the Balanced Universe
Aspect #5: Regenerative Living	Self-Centered, Constrictive Living	Heart-Centered, eXpansive Living
Aspect #6: Learning	Memorizing for the Test	Life-Long Learning
Aspect #7: Wisdom	Wisdom Accumulating with Age	Wisdom Accumulating Through Learning & Experiencing
Aspect #8: Purpose	Living Without Purpose	Living with Purpose

Personal Vision

ESSENCE Aspect	Old-Paradigm, 20th-Century Living	New-Paradigm, 21st-Century Living
Aspect #9: Change	Unwillingness to Change	Embracing of Change
Aspect #10: Heart-Centeredness	Living Mind-Centered Lives	Living Heart-Centered Lives
Aspect #11: Forgiveness	Forgiveness as a Weakness	Forgiveness as a Strength
Aspect #12: Self-Love	Low Self-Love, Narcissism	Infinite Self-Love, Modesty
Aspect #13: God Within	God Residing Out There	God Residing Within Each of Us
Aspect #14: Honesty	Dishonesty Is Tolerated	Honesty Prevails
Aspect #15: Authenticity	Acting a Certain Way to Conform	Simply Being Our Authentic Selves
Aspect #16: Truth	Lying Out of Fear	Truth as Protection

ESSENCE

ESSENCE Aspect	Old-Paradigm, 20th-Century Living	New-Paradigm, 21st-Century Living
Aspect #17: Trust	Trust Having to Be Earned	Trust Being Inherent
Aspect #18: Hope	Hopelessness Dominating	Hopefulness Everywhere
Aspect #19: Faith	Low Faith in One's Self	High Faith in One's Self
Aspect #20: Belief	Low Belief in God/Spirit	High Belief in God/Spirit
Aspect #21: Divine Will	Personal Will Attempting to Force the Desired Outcome	Divine Will Allowing the Desired Outcome
Aspect #22: Patience	Highly Impatient World	Highly Patient World
Aspect #23: Bravery	Living in Fear, with Low Courage	Confronting Our Fears with Bravery
Aspect #24: Perseverance	Determination to Conquer via Our Minds	Inspiration to Action via Our Hearts

ESSENCE Aspect	Old-Paradigm, 20th-Century Living	New-Paradigm, 21st-Century Living
Aspect #25: Fortitude	Avoiding Discomfort	Journeying on with Fortitude
Aspect #26: Gratitude	Having a Low Sense of Gratefulness, Taking for Granted	Being Highly Grateful, Counting Our Blessings Daily
Aspect #27: Humility	Success Breeding Arrogance	Remaining Humble when Successful
Aspect #28: Simplicity	Embracing Materialism	Embracing Simplicity
Aspect #29: Collaboration	Competition Dominating	Collaboration Prevailing
Aspect #30: Mind Energy	Low Understanding of How Our Thoughts and Feelings Create Our Lives	High Understanding of How Our Thoughts and Feelings Create Our Lives
Aspect #31: Body Energy	High Percentage of Obese People, with Bodies NOT Being Our Temples	Low Percentage of Obese People, with Bodies Being Our Temples

ESSENCE

ESSENCE Aspect	Old-Paradigm, 20th-Century Living	New-Paradigm, 21st-Century Living
Aspect #32: Spirit Energy	Low Awareness of Spirit Energy	High Awareness of Spirit Energy
Aspect #33: Present Time	Living in Past and/or Future Time	Living in Present Time
Aspect #34: Vision	Limited Vision	Unlimited Vision
Aspect 35: Focus	Difficulty Focusing due to Stress, Worry, and Doubt	High Sense of Focus, Manifesting Visions
Aspect #36: Contemplation	Low Contemplation and Poor Decisions Amid a Fast-Paced World	High Contemplation and Diligent Decisions Amid a Slower-Paced World
Aspect #37: Acceptance	Low Acceptance, High Discrimination	High Acceptance, Low Discrimination
Aspect #38: Willingness	Fixation on Preconceived Outcomes, Imposing Personal Will to Force Desired Outcomes	Freedom from Preconceived Outcomes, Allowing Divine Will to Determine Desired Outcomes

ESSENCE Aspect	Old-Paradigm, 20th-Century Living	New-Paradigm, 21st-Century Living
Aspect #39: Money Energy	Money as Finite and Scarce	Money as Energy and Abundantly Available
Aspect #40: Compassion	Low Sense of Compassion for Others	High Sense of Compassion for Others
Aspect #41: Give & Receive	Take & Get Mentality	Give & Receive Mentality
Aspect #42: Equality	Inequality, Oppression, Hierarchy, Discrimination	Equality, Freedom, No Hierarchy, No Discrimination
Aspect #43: Unity	Low Sense of Community	High Sense of Community
Aspect #44: Love	Mind-Centered Lives Creating Too Little Love in the World	Heart-Centered Lives Creating a Lot of Love in the World

For a deeper understanding of how to create a meaningful life in the 21st century, we suggest reading the second book in the ESSENCE Trilogy Book Series, *Regenerating Humanity*. This book goes into the details of how to regenerate our lives, experiencing much greater love, joy, freedom, abundance, and peace. RegeneratingHumanity.com.

WE APPRECIATE the time you've invested in reading ESSENCE. Our desire is that this experience has expanded your awareness and broadened your perspective in new and exciting ways, bringing more love, joy, freedom, abundance, and peace into your life!

We'd also greatly appreciate if you'd leave a book review (on Amazon and/or elsewhere) to help other Sleeping Souls, Seekers, and Awakened decide if ESSENCE is a good read for them. ***Will you please help us build awareness by taking action now?***

Also, if inspired, please visit our Web sites:

EXPANSION	21stCenturyParadigm.com
VISION	RegeneratingHumanity.com
CREATION	The21stCenturyAlchemist.com
UNITY	The Harmony Project.org
PUBLISHING	princetongreen.org
ANN'S SITE	AnnEmerson.com
BO'S SITE	BoLockwood.com
ART	OliviArt.gallery
AGENCY	Unfold.com

Many thanks, and have a wonderful journey.

~ Ann and Bo

DAILY AFFIRMATIONS

ESSENCE:
I am committed to my daily practice.

THE FOLLOWING PAGES centralize all the Daily Affirmations so you can easily integrate and reference them in your daily practice. At first, you may feel uncomfortable stating many of the Affirmations. This is simply the discomfort of change.

As these Affirmations gently embed themselves into your subconscious mind, you will begin to consciously believe them, feeling a tremendous sense of inspiration as well as a validation that you are positively changing.

I view the world through an extremely broad perspective.

I am an infinite being accepting from an infinite source.

I am connected as One with all aspects of the Universe.

ESSENCE

*With accurate information,
I live harmoniously in balance.*

*I live in harmony with Nature,
for I am Nature.*

*I continue to learn
throughout my lifetime.*

*I rely on my wisdom to make
the proper choices in life.*

*I am fulfilled by
serving my life's purpose.*

*I am open to, and accept, all changes
that support my life's purpose.*

*I live a heart-centered life,
making heart-centered decisions.*

*I forgive myself and others, as we are all teachers for
one another. Forgiveness is my path to freedom.*

I love myself infinitely.

I am connected to God within me.

I live my life with a pure and honest heart.

I inspire others by being my authentic self.

DAILY AFFIRMATIONS

I live my truth, as it protects me.

I trust myself and others.

My high degree of hope is contagious.

*I have faith that we will transition to
21st-century living, preserving Mother Earth
for the next seven generations.*

I believe in my abilities and myself.

I surrender my personal will to Divine will.

*I listen to the rhythm of my Soul.
And I trust the Creator's pace.*

I live my life with bravery.

*I will continue to persevere on my journey
until I manifest my true heart's desires
and fulfill my life's purpose.*

*I am strong and capable.
And I live my life with grace and ease.*

*I am at peace with myself
and grateful in every area of my life.*

I am humble.

ESSENCE

I live a simple life with very little drama.

*I work in collaboration with others
to help fuel our collective success.*

My mind is filled with positive thoughts.

*The stronger I make my body,
the more energy I can hold and emit.*

I realize who I am: mind, body, spirit, and Soul.

*I live fully in the present and
am open to all possibilities.*

*With vision, everything is possible
and everything is solvable.*

*My focus inspires me
to manifest my vision into reality.*

*I contemplate my thoughts before I act,
to choose the right decisions for my life.*

*I accept myself. I accept the infinite.
I accept I am infinite.*

I willingly accept abundance, without any resistance.

Money is energy. Investing in myself always pays off.

I live my life with compassion for others and myself.

I am fulfilled by giving to others.

I view everyone and everything as equals.

*I am an aspect of the togetherness
that bonds our unified community.*

*I send thoughts of love,
and love returns in overflowing measure.*

I am committed to my daily practice. Namaste.

MY PERSONAL JOURNEY

Ann Emerson

PERHAPS IT WAS MY DYSLEXIA that pointed me the way to my nontraditional path of learning, but I have been at it for 67 years. In doing so, I joined with those communities that were far from the mainstream. I was and still am dedicated to learning and serving life, so I am always embraced as a student, even at the age of 83.

I was never awarded traditional academic credentials, as I dropped out of high school at the age of 17 to join the workforce. I married very young and soon found myself abandoned with three small sons. My passion to learn at that time had much to do with saving my sons from poverty and making a better world for them. I married again four years later and had two more children with my second husband. You could say I learned "on the road," with grit and grace and a passionate drive for my family—and then for families everywhere.

I could share stories about hitting the wall many times over my lifetime. Stories in which I felt totally blocked and then a door would open before me in the most unexpected way. As soon as I saw that door I opened it just as quickly, often with fear, pain, and struggle, knowing these experiences would be important keys to the change I was seeking.

More than 40 years ago I was ordained as an Interfaith Minister by Rabbi Joseph Gelberman at the New Seminary in New York City. I have been director of five interfaith study centers, and I am now director of The Sanctuary of Sophia (a.k.a. The Sanctuary of the Divine Feminine) in Lake Mary, Florida.

Many are the people whose shoulders I stand upon. I hope that ESSENCE will, in turn, help others with their own lives. This is really a short list communities and teachers, and only the most dynamic:

> The Human Potential Movement; the Rebirthing community; the Women's Movement; the Civil Rights Movement and community; the Shalom Mountain community; the Christian Charismatic community; the Kripalu Yoga community; the Omega Institute for Holistic Studies and its community; the Network Community in the New York State Prison System; the MaryEl Angel community; Ken Wilber's Superhuman Operating System and community; Gloria Amendola's mystical community; the Yuen Method of Chinese Energetics community; the Matrix Energetics community; the Tony Robbins community; the Quantum-Touch community; the Access Consciousness community; Pranic Healing by Master Choa Kok Sui; Dr. Michael Cotton and the Higher Brain Living community; Dr. Bradley Nelson's Emotion Code and Body Code community; Dr. Alexander Loyd and the

The Healing Code community; and now, the Regenerating Humanity community with founder Bo Lockwood.

Nine years ago I created a 900-page Web site, www.TheHarmonyProject.org, devoted to 21st-century spiritual paths and the interconnection of those paths toward achieving enlightenment. The major contributors to that community have been Peter van Geldern, Joseph Neumayer, Eric Wenzel, Andrew DiFiore Jr., and Ann Marie Sawicki. To this day we receive thousands of hits monthly, globally.

I have seen the evolution of so many great ideas that were considered bizarre many years ago but are now part of the culture. To name just a few, these are equal rights, meditation, energy healing, honoring Native American wisdom and teachings, interfaith communities, and permaculture communities, which honor and care for Mother Earth.

One of my favorite quotes is by the Dalai Lama: "If you're a good Christian, you're a good Buddhist."

We are living in a time of dynamic change, and "the shifts" are happening more quickly than ever before in human history. I have worked with thousands as students and clients, and been greatly blessed as I have learned so much from all of them. I thank them for their trust and dedication.

The communities and movements I have worked with saw the shortcomings in American culture. They sought to enhance and shift life compassionately, creatively, and with joy, for the sake of healing all the people on Mother Earth, by understanding the interconnectedness of life.

One of my master teachers, Barbara Marx Hubbard, is a visionary, a social innovator. She is an evolutionary thinker who believes that global change happens when we work collectively and selflessly for the greater good. She realizes that the lessons of evolution teach us that problems are evolutionary drivers and that crises precede transformation, giving a new way of seeing and responding to our global situation.

America is wonderful because new ideas are always available to those who seek to make the world better for all.

Ann Emerson
The Sanctuary of Sophia
Lake Mary, Florida

MY PERSONAL JOURNEY

Bo Lockwood

I AM just like most other ordinary Americans. I was born in New Jersey and moved to Pennsylvania at the age of five. We lived in the rural part of the western Philadelphia suburbs, between two awesome neighborhoods. I was raised with a strong work ethic and a true sense of American pride.

My childhood was wonderful; and if you asked my two brothers, I suspect they would say the same. We grew up on skateboards, go-karts, mini bikes, dirt bikes, three-wheelers, fishing boats, trucks, and hot rods. Our dad taught us about engines, construction, electricity, plumbing, you name it, which is why today all three of us can fix and build just about anything. Our mom was always there for us, too.

I grew up with a group of hell-raising friends collectively known as "the boys." We loved pulling pranks, we loved drinking beer, we loved four-wheeling, and we loved our girlfriends. We spent our summer days hanging out at the Jersey Shore.

Long story short, at the age of 15, I was hit hard by my brother's 1967 Mustang, pinning me against a tree. And no, he wasn't behind the wheel; I managed to do it all on my own. I explicitly remember the car as it rolled down the hill toward me, and the panic I felt as I ran vigorously backward trying to get away from it. I recall the tree that put an abrupt end to my retreat, and the fateful impact that painfully followed. As I was standing, pinned against the tree, I quickly resolved to squirm my way out, knowing my skin was going to rip in the process, and it did. I incurred major punctures on my left thigh and calf, and multiple layers of skin on my right calf had torn off.

As I sprawled on the ground, blood spewing everywhere, I felt no pain. Instead, I experienced an extreme sense of calmness, warmth, and light. I was pondering my next move, even though I couldn't move and nobody was home. I watched our neighbor, Mrs. King, ease on by in her green Pinto, oblivious to me lying on the ground in a pool of blood. Our other neighbor, a.k.a. our mom's spy, happened to see the entire event as it transpired. She was crippled, physically incapable of coming to my aid. However, she called Kurt Yeager, our neighbor who happened to be an Eagle Scout; he was able to respond quickly and treat me until the ambulance arrived. To this day, I am grateful for their actions, because otherwise I would have bled to death.

I've recently learned, through an intuitive healer, that this experience has shaped my life, making me who I am today. I was having an out-of-body experience, which explains my sense of calm and light. She expressed that such a traumatic encounter blew open a part of my brain, raising my awareness to an entirely new level. She said that it literally changed the course of my life, leading me right to where I am today.

After high school, I went on to earn my bachelor's degree in finance from Pennsylvania State University. These were among the best years of my life. While there, I became a member of the rugby team, playing for seven seasons. We had excellent coaching and were Division I, top-10 nationally ranked every season. I was honored to be the co-captain my last two seasons and learned more on the pitch than in the classroom, building my character, bravery, perseverance, and fortitude to new heights. My teammates were from England, Scotland, Belgium, Ireland, New Zealand, and South Africa, to name a few. I learned about diversity, camaraderie, leadership, and the meaning of teamwork. Even though we all looked, spoke, and viewed the world differently, as we stepped onto the pitch we were One unified team. We were a tightly bonded group of determined men who had each other's backs. Prior to graduation, I passed the Series 7 exam, becoming certified as a stockbroker.

After graduation, I started dating my future wife, Lisa. We had met briefly at Penn State two years prior on a Spring Break trip to Daytona Beach, Florida, which provided a nice segue for me to reintroduce myself. Throughout our marriage, we encountered many stressful situations, including the growth of our business and my open-heart surgery at the age of 30 to correct a birth defect. Our marriage lasted 12 years, during which time the two most special people in my life were born—our daughters, Hannah and Olivia. Our marriage resulted in the three brightest days of my life—our wedding day and the birth of each of our girls. It also included the darkest days of my life—especially those following our separation. Overall, I am grateful for Lisa, as she has been one of my greatest teachers.

My career path has been rather straightforward. After college, I pursued a career in investment banking before realizing it wasn't for me. Then, with the help of Lisa, I started, built, and sold the largest event rental company in Philadelphia. At our peak, we had 150-plus employees and three warehouses. After selling the company at the age of 32, I moved on to become a Partner with the GALLUP Poll, helping to lead the U.S. Higher Education practice. GALLUP sponsored me to earn my master's degree in leadership from the University of Nebraska. Also while at GALLUP, though, my marriage disintegrated. I hit rock bottom, burned out from the stress, stuff, and debt. I began to seek.

One early morning in September 2008 I awoke with the vision in my mind of founding princetongreen.org. I'm really not sure how it happened; it was just there—the vision, the name of the organization, the culture, the organizational structure, the products, the services, the clients, and the community—all in my mind. I could see the organization in operation. I could feel the engagement of the culture. I could hear people talking about being a part of the Princeton Green community. It all became clear. I just knew this was something I was supposed to do.

I resigned from GALLUP in October 2008, officially founding princetongreen.org that November. I set out on this journey as the economy was collapsing. I'm a contrarian; therefore, I observe the market and do the opposite. Admittedly, though, I didn't think the next seven years would be so very challenging. I assumed the previous four years of separation and divorce were my darkest days. I soon discovered that this wasn't true, as my running a gauntlet through Hell continued.

In 2010, about two years into my spiritual seeking, I met my one business partner, Peter van Geldern. His entrance into my life was both needed and timely. He helped to refine and solidify the princetongreen.org brand. We also published our first book together, *Regenerating America: eXpansive Entrepreneurs Growing the New Energy Economy*.

Peter also introduced me to his mom, Ann Emerson, who is a marvelous woman, very spiritually connected, and a lifelong learner. She comes from the lineage of Ralph Waldo Emerson, and continues to expand her family's legacy of building spiritual awareness. At 83, Ann has more aliveness than most people have in their 40s. I have benefited greatly by her and through her. I have received 43 years of her spiritual knowledge over the past six years, which has changed me in profound ways. I am so grateful that Peter and Ann were brought into my life with Divine timing; I've grown to learn that there are no coincidences.

In 2013, Ann introduced me to Shalom Mountain, a leading-edge retreat and study center for exploring personal growth, relationships, love, the evolution of consciousness on the planet, and what it means to be fully alive. Shalom helped me heal on many levels.

In 2014, I discovered shamanism, being introduced to monthly full-moon fire ceremonies with Shaman Candy. Shamanism is the world's oldest spiritual practice and cannot really be considered a religion because it has no dogma, no organization, no sacred book, and no recognized leader; nor does it have a single founder. Essentially, shamanism is embodying the elemental powers of Nature.

In 2015, I went on my first shamanic journey in the Amazon jungle, experiencing three consecutive Ayahuasca ceremonies, which involved facing my fears and healing past traumas. I returned home a different person, having an open heart and experiencing greater love, joy, and peace in my life.

I continue to practice shamanism, meeting wonderful people while discovering new aspects of myself. On a recent journey, I met my "shamanic family," including my granddad, dad, two sisters, three nieces and one nephew, along with my best friend and neighbor. We all grew up together approximately 300 years ago!

Before I became a **Seeker**, my faith and belief waffled. I wanted to believe, I kind of believed, and therefore I didn't believe. What I've learned is that it took bravery for me to begin seeking. As I started traversing, my awareness expanded and my perspective broadened. My bravery morphed into faith. And once I reached a certain altitude on my ascent, believing and knowing just happened. My story instantly changed, and this is when I truly discovered my life's purpose—helping people discover a new pathway leading to 21st-century living. I have a knowing that I will not die in this chapter of my infinite life until my purpose has been fulfilled. Nor do I know whether any information is even accurate. What I do know is that by me living my life with greater awareness of all of the Aspects of ESSENCE as they relate to myself, I have greater love, joy, freedom, abundance, and peace in my life; which is why I desire to share it with everyone else.

I don't consider myself **Awakened**, even though my Soul is much more awake. I am a **Seeker**, as I have more to learn before I arrive at a place of wholeness. I don't view myself as being special. I am simply a living Soul, just like you, occupying this body in this chapter of my infinite journey. Where we may differ is that I have learned to live my life by effectively managing fear and stepping into my infinite power; yet so can you.

Overall, I'm in a great place. My mind is clear, my heart open, and my body strong, while I am sleeping well, eating healthily, and living in the Divine flow. I've learned that materialism to build up one's ego is a bunch of bullshit. I now have a simple and fulfilling life with inner peace. I've grown to fully accept and love who I am—an infinite spiritual being having a human experience. And, in this human experience, I have meaningfully re-generated my life spiritually, physically, psychologically, emotionally, and economically.

I am so excited for what is yet to come. I used to fear the unknown, and now I love it. Every day brings with it a new surprise.

Bo Lockwood
The Treehouse

ACKNOWLEDGMENTS

Ann Emerson

MY GRATITUDE AND THANKS go to my five children and their spouses for supporting their wild mom. Thank you, Jack and Jody van Geldern, Steve and Anne van Geldern, Phil and Margaret van Geldern, Alicia Braccia, and Peter and Joan van Geldern. I am constantly learning from you!

To my grandchildren, Sean van Geldern, Emily van Geldern, Abby van Geldern, Kate and Mike Bowler, Mara van Geldern, Pete van Geldern, Kendall Braccia, Shannah van Geldern, Ben van Geldern, and Josh van Geldern: What a dynamic generation! Experiencing you, my heart opens to love and *mind-seeking-truth* and service to the *Light*! You have no concept what life in America was like in the 1930s and 1940s, and that is a very good thing! You are the change-makers now, and in the near future the next generation will arise from you. WOW!

To my first great grandchild, Jane Emerson Bowler, who arrived this January. We welcome you to our family.

I want to thank Bo Lockwood for our work together over the past seven years. Without this deep partnership in learning and serving the *Light*, this book would not have been published. This is just the beginning of many new and wonderful adventures in learning and serving that we will have together. We are blessed to be an integral part of the positive change in our culture. We aim to leave a beneficial legacy, certainly here in America and possibly the world, as we are truly a global community now.

To my "Luminaries" I send my love: Matthew Fox, Jean Huston, Gloria Steinem, the Dalai Lama, Father Thomas Keating, Rabbi Joseph Gelberman, Rupert Sheldrake, Martin Luther King Jr., Dr. Gerald J. Jud, Margaret Starbird, Ken Wilber, Barbara Marx Hubbard, Gregg Braden, and Tony Robbins.

Finally, to quote Albert Einstein: "Our task must be to free ourselves by widening our circle of compassion to embrace all living creatures and the whole of nature and its beauty."

~ Ann

ACKNOWLEDGMENTS

Bo Lockwood

I THANK MY DAUGHTERS, Hannah and Olivia, as well as my parents and family for sticking by me through my most darkest days. You taught me the meaning of unconditional love. I am grateful.

I thank Ann Emerson, my coauthor and spiritual mentor, who has helped expand my awareness and broaden my perspective on life, people, the Earth, and the Universe. I wouldn't be where I am today without you. I am grateful.

I thank Rita Elizabeth Garcia, my Amazon jungle angel, who helped me more fully open my heart, face my fears, and awaken my inspiration. Your air helped to ignite my fire. I am grateful.

I thank Dana Lichtstrahl, Hala G. Stephan, and Elizabeth Ely for our deep friendships, helping to expand me and our work together. I am grateful.

I thank Alyona Bauer for experiencing the pureness of your love. Your water helps to balance my fire. You are amazing. I am grateful.

I thank my Soul brother, Peter van Geldern, for designing the trilogy book covers. I am grateful.

I thank my Soul brother, Gerry St. Onge, for all of the triggering times. I am grateful.

I thank Lisa Furlong for being the loving and devoted mother of our daughters, as well as being among my greatest teachers. I am grateful.

I thank our two dogs, Nikki and Hazel, for teaching me the meaning of devotion. I am grateful.

I thank "the boys," as our crazy times somehow shaped the person I am today—Andy Pancoast, Bud Haly, Tom McDevitt, Drew Taylor, Joe DelViscio, John Amen, Danny Parker, Frank DeRobertis, Gary Ramondo, Darius Murray, Fran Conway, Patrick Sweet, Paul Rippy, Steve Toolan, Dave Able, Norman Aker, Jimmy Colleran, Paul Gluck, Marty Friel, George Rambo, Bill Meredith, Jim Beltz, Kevin Parker, Barry Cox, Gary Birchall, John Perrotta, George Vance, Paul Perry, Mark Noble, Jim Baxter, Tom Coughlin, Billy Coyle, Frank Tropho, Bill Pommerer, Jimmy McDevitt, Jay Beaver, Darrin DelViscio, Michael McDevitt, Rob Coughlin, Evans Pancoast, and Gary King. I am grateful.

I thank my Penn State friends, as my time in State College was among the most transformative years of my life—Dee Bergbauer, Dave Huff, George Felt, Bill Coccagna, Katie Bergbauer, John Taylor, Ken Kovalchuk, Jeff Bischer, Scott Seifried, Stevie Rae, Lenny Dore, Tim Nestor, Thad Picklo, Herman Delang, Mike Campbell, Steve Luttmann, Mike Donahue, Doug Ziegler, Kimo Hollingsworth, Lance Polcyn, J.D. Hayes, Mike Grigor, Frazer Grigor, Andy MacDonald, Adrian Smith, and the balance of my rugby teammates, including Marti, Al, Ben, Nigel, Kevin, Doug, and Truck. I am grateful.

I thank my GALLUP friends, as my working there was the best leadership development experience so far in this chapter of my infinite life—Jennifer Ross, Neli Esipova, Lori Stohs, Alec Gallup, Rajesh Srinivasan, Ellen Hoeppner, Mike van Buskirk, John McNee, Donna Chlopak, John Fleming, Bev Passerella, Jeannie Hepp, Connie Rath, Barry Conchie, Jacque Murphy, Jim Clifton, Jim Kreiger, Larry Emond, Randy Beck, Curt Coffman, Tim Hodges, Todd Johnson, Jacque Merritt, Tosca Lee, Jan Miller, Joe Struer, Cheryl Beamer, Adam Pressman, Charlie Colon, Mark Turner, Jessica Winter, Tamara Sniffen, Gus MacGyver, Mark Miller, Bruce Wilson, Bob Goodwin, Dave French, Charles Garcia, and AJ Scribante. I am grateful.

I thank my princetongreen.org friends for a wild roller coaster ride coming in for a safe landing—Kirven Talone, Nancy Bogle St. John, Curry Smith, Glenn Massamillo, Vic Patalano, Ben Duncan, Karen Nathan, Rees Keck, Tim Razzaq, Dave Peters, David Amico, John DiNenna, John Henry, Mark Swiger, Brian Preski, Andy Kern, Yaron Kaminski, Richard McLaughlin, Michael Murphy, Vern Reo, Janice Hall, Ross Wishnick, Kelly Boyd, David Welsh, Jason Ulshafer, Michael Talone, and Kacy Talone. I am grateful.

I thank my yoga friends for helping to open me up—Katra Longsdorf, Susan Sprecher, Elle Kaplan, Laura Rothstein, Maria Campbell, Cathy Armstrong Frank, Alison Gilheany, Kim Aubrey, Darla Lux, Carrie Robb, Bob Sasson, Fiona Yohannan, Carolyn

Jensen, Erin Cleary Cook, Mike Goodguy, and Molly Mitnick.

I thank my Shalom Mountain friends for helping to heal my Soul—Edie Tirpak, Nance McGee, Vyana Bergen, Jeff Hilliard, Cristian Graca, Carrie Jameson, Meg Rayne, Shelly Reichenbach, Jon Terrell, Mark Monchek, Naz Fontanilla, Mark Alexandru, John Ellsworth, Judi Johnston, Jenny Mark, Clara Duhon, Rosemary Tarcza, Susan Lamprecht, Lindsay Kochen, Barbara DeCesare, and Alex York. I am grateful.

I thank my Soulutions for Daily Living and A Course in Miracles friends for being part of a wonderful local spiritual community—Honey Bellosi, Mark Van der Gaag, Wade Batterton, Sam Schnell, Randi Forman, Carol Dannin, Michael Giancarli, Meghan Lemli, Maya Kauffman Rapine, Kevin Giang, BobbyLight Rowlands, Terri Polefka, Terry Engelmann, Patty Hritz, Johannah Batterton, Maureen Groetsch, and Linda Hill. I am grateful.

I thank my shamanic community friends for helping me face my fears, expand myself, and heal—Candy Batterton, Kate Laking, Linda Fitch, Luz Moyer, Mike Peluso, Kathy Vervan Bugglin, Genevieve Frances, Natalie Elisha, Lee Schwalb, Brad Oliphant, Iris Reif, David Reif, Larry Forsblad, Sarah Rubin, Mary Nahra, Beth Nolan, Steven Lichtscheidl, Steve Bugglin, Saharra White-Wolf, Markus Skand, Penny Goldmuntz, Michael Trachman, Jessica Zhong, Glenn Nuttall, Jane Herrmann, Sara Shafer, Melanie Thompson, and

Cherilyn Hopkins, Joyce Smile, and Anna Circlehands. I am grateful.

I thank my LBNA friends for being a great network of business folks to connect with—Jen Kine Clark, Tom Dingwall, Tom Ruhfass, Ebbe Skoval, Chuck Addis, Shayna Carnevale, Joe Ramagli, Mark Kronberger, Scott Mitchell, Jackie Veasley, Lonny Boline, Steve Rodriguez, Jeff Sibner, Jacqui Fedele, Carol Woytus, Scott Melzer, Doug Sce, Craig Turet, Jonni Bankert, Kent Hodgert, Bill D'Arcy, Peter Bondarkenko, and Patrick Clark.

I thank my friends at thyssenkrupp Elevator, Local 5, and 1515 Market Street for being on the bridge to where I am going next—Cameron Worley, Lou Pilic, Manny Estevez, Tony Polidori, Valerie Ponzo, Pam Williams, Shawn Suter, Rose Nowon, Dennis Millington, Malika Muhammad, Ozena Dixon, Bruce O'Donnell, Glenn McNatt, Tim Verzella, Jim Delgado, Dylan Todd, Jim Schanne, Danny Goral, Bob Stewart, Steve Sender, Jim Stowman, Al Wittenberger, Jacquelyn Austin, Amanda McConnell, Kelly Bieler, Adam Luckey, Maura McGovern-O'Shea, Ed Rutland, Kevin Burkett, Andy Pannell, Brian Bowler, Bill Russo, Doug DeMarco, Gene Keehfus, Steve Waters, Jake Hogan, Mike Butts, Jake Twombly, Don Welsh, Tony Rice, Joe O'Connor, John Schroeder, Bruce Haines, Eddie Yeager, George Hoenstien, Dave McAdams, Jim Chorney, Bill Walthes, John Horner, Ed Loomis, Bill Johnston, Joe Williams, Jack Koch, Keli Wallace, Kathy Palmer, and Kelly Hillis. I am grateful.

ESSENCE

I thank various friends, all of whom have supported me in some way on my spiritual journey —Arlene Rose Curley, Jean-Michel Tournier, Larry Greene, Steve Swaim, MaryLynn Schiavi, Wendy Worth, Jake Lichtstrahl, Jodi Stevens, Scott Stevens, Grant Captanian, Seth Goldberg, Anna Burke, Jacqueline Sundy, Patty Alfonso, Nicole Bello, Sheila McDonnell, Monica Malpass, Gina Rouse, Kristy Cardellio, Christopher Zelov, John Raatz, Nick Ligidakis, Barbara Heinemann, Robert Phoenix, Susan Kerr, Stan Silverman, Paul Furlong, Nancy Jensen, Jon Jensen, Tara Rountree, Mindy Knapp, Sandra McGill, Lisa Gruenloh, Richard Roger, Carolanne Anselmo, Theresa Ogier, Erika Brandsma, Dorea Dugan, Larry Dugan, Barbara Simmons, Lisa Shelby-Glick, Ken Glick, Jill Kinsella LeClair, Rick Baldassari, Ric Breines, Max Thornburg, Cindy del Rosario, Victoria Klejmont, Connie Denham, Ursula Gelleri, Alex Gelleri, and Shaun Serbay. I am grateful.

I thank my 52nd-birthday University of Miami 'U' friends and my daughters for an amazing week, capping it off at the full moon drum circle on Miami Beach—Sarah Capraro, Kurt Daum, Faryn Solomon, Katherine Dudzinsky, Vanessa Serure, Bailey Bingham, and Sarah Zoeller. I am grateful.

Lastly, I thank Spirit for supporting me in doing my inner work of awakening my sleeping Soul. I have released my past, am fully present, and open to the future. I live in the unknown. I am grateful.

~ Bo

GLOSSARY

20th-century living: A term used to describe living in the old paradigm of worry, doubt, oppression, scarcity, and turmoil, while living in opposition to Nature. Also referred to as constrictive living or mind-centered living.

21st-century living: A term used to describe living in the new paradigm of love, joy, freedom, abundance, and peace, while living in harmony with Nature. Analogous to regenerative living, which includes an Earthly existence of continuous improvement. Also referred to as eXpansive living or heart-centered living.

Acceptance (Aspect #37): Avoiding moral judgments.

Authenticity (Aspect #15): Fully embracing our genuine selves, thus remaining true to who we really are.

Awakened: A term used to describe a person who is living in the new paradigm, viewing the world with unlimited vision, being open to all possibilities.

Awareness: Our perception of a situation, which dictates our perspective on life.

Balance (Aspect #4): An even distribution of weight enabling someone or something to remain upright and steady.

Belief (Aspect #20): An acceptance that a statement is true or that something exists.

Body energy (Aspect #31): A term used to describe a state of existence whereby our bodies are our temples, and the greater care we have for our temples, the more body energy we can hold.

Bravery (Aspect #23): Courageous behavior or character.

Change (Aspect #9): To make or become different.

Collaboration (Aspect #29): The action of working with someone to produce or create something.

Constrictive awareness: A term used to describe a mindset that places limits on our infinite potential and operates from an old paradigm, or belief system, that we are separate from Nature and separate from each other.

Constrictive living: A term used to describe living in the old paradigm of fear, worry, doubt, scarcity, competition, prestige, power, control, materialism, and other negative attributes. Also referred to as the old paradigm of 20th-century living.

Constrictive path: A term used to describe a way of life whereby we continue the old way of doing things because we believe it will return us to a place of prosperity. Those traveling this path will be repeating past mistakes, engaging in destructive behaviors, and continuing to deplete the Earth's resources. The ultimate outcome of living on this path is *Civilization Dies*.

Compassion (Aspect #40): The sympathetic concern for the sufferings or misfortunes of others.

Connectedness (Aspect #3): To bring together or into contact so that a real or notional link is established.

Contemplation (Aspect #36): The action of looking thoughtfully at something for a long time; deep reflective thought.

Daily affirmation: A statement that affirms one's beliefs daily. In the context of the ESSENCE, affirmations are statements that affirm a belief in one's Self in the new paradigm of 21st-century living, through repeating the statement to one's Self on a daily basis. Over time, the affirmation becomes embedded in the subconscious mind, influencing the way one's Self naturally thinks about, believes in, and perceives life.

Decision time: A term used to describe whether one is willing to decide to change. In the context of ESSENCE, this is the decision to change one's life

ESSENCE

from living in the old paradigm in order to traverse to the new paradigm.

Divine will (Aspect #21): A term used to describe a belief in God having a plan for humanity.

Equality (Aspect #42): The state of being equal, especially in status, rights, and opportunities.

eXpansive awareness: A term used to describe an individual who views the world through a lens of the infinite. Their awareness of the Universe, the Earth, and human identity is extremely eXpansive, and their perspective is extremely broad. They believe that with vision, everything is possible and everything is solvable.

eXpansive living: A term used to describe living in the new paradigm of love, joy, freedom, abundance, and peace, while living in harmony with Nature. Analogous to the new paradigm of 21st-century living. Also referred to as regenerative living or heart-centered living.

eXpansive path: A path to our new existence leading us to 21st-century living. Living on the eXpansive path means living an infinite existence, free of fear, full of love. The ultimate outcome of living on this path is *Civilization Thrives*.

Faith (Aspect #19): Complete trust or confidence in someone or something.

Focus (Aspect #35): The act of concentrating interest or activity on something.

Forgiveness (Aspect #11): The action or process of forgiving or being forgiven.

Fortitude (Aspect #25): Having courage in a situation of pain and/or adversity.

Future time: A term used to describe a state of existence focused on future illusions.

Giving & Receiving (Aspect #41): In the highest sense, to give is to freely offer something valuable to another. To receive is to accept what is being given with gratitude and humility.

God within (Aspect #13): A term used to describe a belief that there is a spark of God within each and every one of us.

Gratitude (Aspect #26): The quality of being thankful; readiness to show appreciation for, and to return, kindness.

Humility (Aspect #27): A modest view of one's own importance—humbleness.

Heart-centeredness (Aspect #10): Having my heart as the focal element of my life.

Heart-centered living: A term used to describe living in the new paradigm of love, joy, freedom, abundance, and peace, as decisions become heart-centered and take into consideration the impact on the next seven generations. Analogous to regenerative living, which includes an Earthly existence of continuous improvement and living in harmony with Nature. Also referred to as 21st-century living or eXpansive living.

Honesty (Aspect #14): The act of being free of deceit and untruthfulness.

Hope (Aspect #18): A feeling of expectation and desire for a certain thing to happen.

Infinite Being (Aspect #2): Limitless or endless in space, extent, or size; impossible to measure or calculate. Infinite existence produces infinite opportunity. When the greater knowledge of the infinite comes to us, we are changed forever, as all limitations are released.

Learning (Aspect #6): The acquisition of knowledge or skills through experience, practice, study, or being taught.

Love (Aspect #44): An intense feeling of deep affection.

Mind energy (Aspect #30): A term used to describe the strength and vitality required for sustained mental activity.

Money energy (Aspect #39): A term used to describe money as a medium of energetic exchange.

Paradigm: A typical example, a pattern, a model.

Past time: A term used to describe a state of existence focused on past memories.

Present time (Aspect #33): A term used to describe a state of existence focused on the present.

Patience (Aspect #22): The capacity to accept or tolerate delay, trouble, or suffering without becoming angry or upset.

Perseverance (Aspect #24): Doing something despite difficulty and/or delay in achieving success.

Perspective: A particular way of regarding something, or a point of view.

Purpose (Aspect #8): The reason for which something is done or created, or for which something exists.

Resistance: The refusal to accept or comply with something; the attempt to prevent something by action or argument.

Regeneration: The action or process of regenerating or being regenerated; continuous improvement.

Regenerative living (Aspect #5): A term used to describe the transition our entire world needs to make in order to live in harmony with Nature. This transition is not for convenience. Rather, it's a matter of survival. At its essence, regenerative living is analogous to the Japanese term *Kaizen*, which means improvement or change for the better, otherwise known as continuous improvement. Those engaged in regenerative living make heart-centered decisions, taking into consideration the impact on the next seven generations (a.k.a. heart-centered living and 21st-century living).

Seeker: A term used to describe a person who is traversing to the new paradigm of 21st-century living.

Self-awareness (Aspect #1): Conscious knowledge of one's own character, feelings, intentions, and desires.

Self-love (Aspect #12): An intense feeling of deep affection for one's Self.

Simplicity (Aspect #28): The quality or condition of being easy to understand or do.

Sleeping Soul: A term used to describe a person who is trapped in the old paradigm of 20th-century living, where the mass of the world population currently resides.

GLOSSARY

Spirit energy (Aspect #32): A term used to describe a state of existence wherein spirit energy is infinite energy. A strong body with a strong heart connects us to this powerful and limitless energy.

Temperance: Moderation or self-restraint, especially in eating and drinking.

Trust (Aspect #17): Acceptance of the truth of a statement without evidence or investigation.

Truth (Aspect #16): That which is true or in accordance with fact or reality.

Traverse: To cross a hill or mountain by means of a series of sideways movements from one line of ascent or descent to another.

Unity (Aspect #43): The state of being united or joined as a whole, as One.

Vision (Aspect #34): The ability to think about or plan the future with imagination and/or wisdom.

Willingness (Aspect #38): In a spiritual context, the practice of remaining open to, and accepting, all opportunities that serve our highest good.

Wisdom (Aspect #7): The quality of having experience, knowledge, and good judgment; the quality of being wise.

REFERENCES

Introduction:
"Children of the Rainbow." Available at: http://sun-nation.org/sun-rainbow-prophecy.html. Accessed October 28, 2012.

Curley, Arlene Rose. *Completing the Seven*. Quakertown: Philosophical Publishing Company, 2012.

Self-Awareness (Aspect #1):
Teilhard de Chardin, Pierre. "Pierre Teilhard de Chardin Quotes." Available at: https://www.brainyquote.com/quotes/quotes/p/pierreteil160888.html. Accessed July 8, 2017.

Sams, Jamie. *The Sacred Path Workbook*. New York: HarperOne, 1991.

Infinite Being (Aspect #2):
Edison, Thomas A. "Thomas A. Edison - Famous Quotes." Available at: http://www.quoteopia.com/famous.php?quotesby=thomasaedison. Accessed February 19, 2013.

Sams, Jamie. *The Sacred Path Workbook*. New York: HarperOne, 1991.

Connectedness (Aspect #3):
Seattle, Chief. "Native American Indian Wisdom Quotes." Available at: http://www.sapphyr.net/natam/quotes-nativeamerican.htm. Accessed February 19, 2013.

Anthony, Robert. "The Secret of Deliberate Creation." Available at: http://hop.clickbank.net/?mind2013/tsdc1129&x=money magnet. Accessed December 19, 2012.

Lockwood, Robert and Peter van Geldern. *Regenerating America*. Scottsdale: Inkwell Productions, 2013.

"Mahatma Gandhi Quotes." Available at: http://thinkexist.com/quotation/earth_provides_enough_to_satisfy_every_mans_need/181709.html. Accessed February 19, 2013.

Sams, Jamie. *The Sacred Path Workbook*. New York: HarperOne, 1991.

Balance (Aspect #4):
Merton, Thomas. "Balanced Life Quotes." Available at: http://www.essentiallifeskills.net/balancedlifequotes.html. Accessed February 19, 2013.

Anthony, Robert. "The Secret of Deliberate Creation." Available at: http://www.21stcenturyliving.org/our-community/education/deliberate-creation/ Accessed December 19, 2012.

Sams, Jamie. *The Sacred Path Workbook*. New York: HarperOne, 1991.

Regenerative Living (Aspect #5):
Kennedy, John F. "BrainyQuote." Available at: http://www.brainyquote.com/quotes/quotes/j/johnfkenn121400.html. Accessed February 19, 2013.

Sams, Jamie. *The Sacred Path Workbook*. New York: HarperOne, 1991.

Learning (Aspect #6):
Edith, Ann (Tomlin, Lily). "Education Quotes." Available at: http://www.etni.org.il/quotes/education.htm. Accessed February 19, 2013.

Sams, Jamie. *The Sacred Path Workbook*. New York: HarperOne, 1991.

REFERENCES

Wisdom (Aspect #7):
Plutarch. "Wisdom Quotes." Available at: http:/www.wisdomquotes.com/quote/plutarch.html. Accessed February 19, 2013.

"Urban Dictionary - Top Definition of old Soul." Available at: http://www.urbandictionary.com/define.php?term=old%20soul. Accessed July 6, 2017.

Sams, Jamie. *The Sacred Path Workbook*. New York: HarperOne, 1991.

Purpose (Aspect #8):
Theresa, Mother. "BrainyQuote." Available at: http://www.brainyquote.com/quotes/quotes/m/mothertere121243.html. Accessed February 19, 2013.

Gruenloh, Lisa. "Purpose Journey." Available at: http://www.purposejourney.com/. Accessed December 19, 2012.

Sams, Jamie. *The Sacred Path Workbook*. New York: HarperOne, 1991.

Change (Aspect #9):
Groeschel, Craig. "I Decided to Start." Available at: http://www.lifechurch.tv/watch/my-story/1. Accessed February 19, 2013.

Sams, Jamie. *The Sacred Path Workbook*. New York: HarperOne, 1991.

Heart-Centeredness (Aspect #10):
Gandhi, Mahatma. "BrainyQuote." Available at: http://www.brainyquote.com/quotes/quotes/m/mahatmagan403952.html. Accessed February 19, 2013.

Anselmo, Carolanne. "Moving Ego from Mind to Heart." Available at: http://www.HealingEnergyAndLearning.com. Accessed February 19, 2013.

Sams, Jamie. *The Sacred Path Workbook*. New York: HarperOne, 1991.

Forgiveness (Aspect #11):
Beecher, Henry Ward. "BrainyQuote." Available at: http://www.brainyquote.com/quotes/quotes/h/henrywardb105212.html. Accessed February 19, 2013.

Sams, Jamie. *The Sacred Path Workbook*. New York: HarperOne, 1991.

Self-Love (Aspect #12):
Stormwolf, Alison "Inspirational Wisdom Quotes on Self-Worth, Self-Love, Self-Esteem." Available at: http://www.soul-awakening.com/quotes/quotes-self-worth.htm. Accessed February 19, 2013.

Sams, Jamie. *The Sacred Path Workbook*. New York: HarperOne, 1991.

God Within (Aspect #13):
Fillmore, Charles. "Charles Fillmore Quote." Available at: http://www.great-quotes.com/quote/56497. Accessed February 19, 2013.

Sams, Jamie. *The Sacred Path Workbook*. New York: HarperOne, 1991.

Honesty (Aspect #14):
"Quotations about Honesty." Available at: http://www.quotegarden.com/honesty.html. Accessed February 19, 2013.

Johnson, Steve. "Is Honesty the Best Policy?" Available at: http://www.insightforliving.ca/insights/october-2012/honesty-best-policy.html. Accessed December 19, 2012.

Sams, Jamie. *The Sacred Path Workbook*. New York: HarperOne, 1991.

REFERENCES

Authenticity (Aspect #15):
Garland, Judy. "BrainyQuote." Available at: http://www.brainyquote.com/quotes/quotes/j/judygarlan104276.html. Accessed February 19, 2013.

Sams, Jamie. *The Sacred Path Workbook*. New York: HarperOne, 1991.

Truth (Aspect #16):
"Truth Quotes." Available at: http://www.tentmaker.org/Quotes/truthquotes.htm. Accessed February 19, 2013.

Sams, Jamie. *The Sacred Path Workbook*. New York: HarperOne, 1991.

Trust (Aspect #17):
Blattner, Jerome. "Trust Quotes and Sayings." Available at: http://www.coolnsmart.com/trust_quotes/. Accessed February 19, 2013.

Sams, Jamie. *The Sacred Path Workbook*. New York: HarperOne, 1991.

Hope (Aspect #18):
Brown, Jackson, Jr., "BrainyQuote." Available at: https://www.brainyquote.com/quotes/quotes/h/hjacksonb629141.html. Accessed July 8, 2017.

Lockwood, Robert and Peter van Geldern. *Regenerating America*. Scottsdale: Inkwell Productions, 2013.

Lopez, Shane J. "How to Bridge the Generational Hope Divide." Available at: http://thegallupblog.gallup.com. Accessed December 19, 2012.

Sams, Jamie. *The Sacred Path Workbook*. New York: HarperOne, 1991.

Faith (Aspect #19):
King, Jr., Martin Luther. "BrainyQuote." Available at: http://www.brainyquote.com/quotes/quotes/m/martinluth105087.html. Accessed February 19, 2013.

Sams, Jamie. *The Sacred Path Workbook*. New York: HarperOne, 1991.

Belief (Aspect #20):
Roosevelt, Eleanor. "Quotes About Faith and Belief." Available at: http://quitsmoking.about.com/od/motivational/a/faithquotations.htm. Accessed February 19, 2013.

Choudhury, Bikram. "Bikram Yoga Class Learning." Available at: http://bikramyogaexton.com. Accessed March 1, 2013.

Sams, Jamie. *The Sacred Path Workbook*. New York: HarperOne, 1991.

Divine Will (Aspect #21):
Emerson, Ralph Waldo. "BrainyQuote." Available at: http://www.brainyquote.com/quotes/quotes/r/ralphwaldo118592.html. Accessed February 19, 2013.

Sams, Jamie. *The Sacred Path Workbook*. New York: HarperOne, 1991.

Patience (Aspect #22):
Tzu, Lao. "Simplicity Quotes." Available at: http://sourcesofinsight.com/simplicity-quotes/. Accessed February 19, 2013.

Sams, Jamie. *The Sacred Path Workbook*. New York: HarperOne, 1991.

Bravery (Aspect #23):
Thucydides. "Thucydides quotes." Available at: http://thinkexist.com/quotation/the_bravest_are_surely_those_who_have_the/12163.html. Accessed February 19, 2013.

Sams, Jamie. *The Sacred Path Workbook*. New York: HarperOne, 1991.

Perseverance (Aspect #24):
"Philosiblog." Available at: http://philosiblog.com/2012/12/19/fall-seven-times-stand-up-eight/. Accessed February 19, 2013.

Sams, Jamie. *The Sacred Path Workbook*. New York: HarperOne, 1991.

Fortitude (Aspect #25):
Mills, Billy. "The Four Virtues." Available at: http://www.runcrn.com/. Accessed February 19, 2013.

Sams, Jamie. *The Sacred Path Workbook*. New York: HarperOne, 1991.

Gratitude (Aspect #26):
Epictetus. "Gratitude Quotes." Available at: http://www.abundance-and-happiness.com/gratitude-quotes.html. Accessed February 19, 2013.

Sams, Jamie. *The Sacred Path Workbook*. New York: HarperOne, 1991.

Humility (Aspect #27):
Temple, William. "Quotations about Humility." Available at: http://www.quotegarden.com/humility.html. Accessed February 19, 2013.

Sams, Jamie. *The Sacred Path Workbook*. New York: HarperOne, 1991.

Simplicity (Aspect #28):
da Vinci, Leonardo. "Simplicity Quotes." Available at: http://sourcesofinsight.com/simplicity-quotes/. Accessed February 19, 2013.

Sams, Jamie. *The Sacred Path Workbook*. New York: HarperOne, 1991.

Collaboration (Aspect #29):
"Divide The Task With Teamwork." Available at: http://www.mdlab.org/news-events/teamwork-divides-the-task-and-multiplies-the-success. Accessed July 9, 2017.

Sams, Jamie. *The Sacred Path Workbook*. New York: HarperOne, 1991.

Mind Energy (Aspect #30):
Baba, Sai. "BrainyQuote." Available at: http://www.brainyquote.com/quotes/quotes/s/saibaba184097.html. Accessed February 19, 2013.

Anthony, Robert. "The Secret of Deliberate Creation." Available at: http://www.21stcenturyliving.org/our-community/education/deliberate-creation/ Accessed December 19, 2012.

Sams, Jamie. *The Sacred Path Workbook*. New York: HarperOne, 1991.

Body Energy (Aspect #31):
Socrates. "BrainyQuote." Available at: http://www.brainyquote.com/quotes/quotes/s/socrates385762.html. Accessed February 19, 2013.

Ochs, Carol. "The Percent of Obese People in the World." Available at: http://www.livestrong.com/article/352574-the-percent-of-obese-people-in-the-world/. Accessed February 19, 2013.

"What percentage of the world's population is overweight?" Available at: http://wiki.answers.com/Q/What_percentage_of_the_world%27s_population_is_overweight. Accessed February 19, 2013.

Sams, Jamie. *The Sacred Path Workbook*. New York: HarperOne, 1991.

Spirit Energy (Aspect #32):
Plato. "BrainyQuote." Available at: http:/www.brainyquote.com/quotes/quotes/p/plato121792.html. Accessed February 19, 2013.

Curley, Arlene Rose. *Completing the Seven*. Quakertown: Philosophical Publishing Company, 2012.

Sams, Jamie. *The Sacred Path Workbook*. New York: HarperOne, 1991.

Present Time (Aspect #33):
Buddha. "BrainyQuote." Available at: http://www.brainyquote.com/quotes/quotes/b/buddha101052.html. Accessed February 19, 2013.

"Who invented time?" Available at: http://answers.yahoo.com/question/index?qid=20061120084401AAL9TXq. Accessed February 19, 2013.

Sams, Jamie. *The Sacred Path Workbook*. New York: HarperOne, 1991.

Vision (Aspect #34):
Hepburn, Audrey. "BrainyQuote." Available at: http://www.brainyquote.com/quotes/quotes/a/audreyhepb413479.html. Accessed February 19, 2013.

Sams, Jamie. *The Sacred Path Workbook*. New York: HarperOne, 1991.

Focus (Aspect #35):
Anderson, Greg. "BrainyQuote." Available at: https://www.brainyquote.com/quotes/quotes/g/greganders132548.html. Accessed July 9, 2017.

Contemplation (Aspect #36):
Dhammapada, The. "My Favorite Contemplation Quotes." Available at: http://healingspiritbodywork.com/contemplationquotes.html. Accessed February 19, 2013.

Sams, Jamie. *The Sacred Path Workbook*. New York: HarperOne, 1991.

Acceptance (Aspect #37):
Whitman, Walt. "BrainyQuote." Available at: http://www.brainyquote.com/quotes/quotes/w/waltwhitma146892.html. Accessed February 19, 2013.

Sams, Jamie. *The Sacred Path Workbook*. New York: HarperOne, 1991.

Willingness (Aspect #38):
Marley, Bob. "Bob Marley Quote." Available at: http://www.great-quotes.com/quote/6718. Accessed February 19, 2013.

Sams, Jamie. *The Sacred Path Workbook*. New York: HarperOne, 1991.

Money Energy (Aspect #39):
Franklin, Benjamin. "Brainy Quote." Available at: https://www.brainyquote.com/quotes/quotes/b/benjaminfr141119.html. Accessed July 9, 2017.

Sams, Jamie. *The Sacred Path Workbook*. New York: HarperOne, 1991.

Compassion (Aspect #40):
Lama, Dalai. "Dalai Lama Quotes." Available at: http://www.brainyquote.com/quotes/quotes/d/dalailama105551.html. Accessed February 19, 2013.

Sams, Jamie. *The Sacred Path Workbook*. New York: HarperOne, 1991.

Giving & Receiving (Aspect #41):
Young, Brigham. "BrainyQuote." Available at: http://www.brainyquote.com/quotes/quotes/b/brighamyou146731.html. Accessed February 19, 2013.

Sams, Jamie. *The Sacred Path Workbook*. New York: HarperOne, 1991.

Equality (Aspect #42):
Becque, Henry. "Equality Quotes." Available at:http://www.finestquotes.com/quote-id-13836.htm. Accessed July 9, 2017.

Sams, Jamie. *The Sacred Path Workbook*. New York: HarperOne, 1991.

Unity (Aspect #43):
Aesop. "Inspirational Quotes by Aesop." Available at: https://www.values.com/inspirational-quotes/4371-in-union-there-is-strength. Accessed July 9, 2017.

Sams, Jamie. *The Sacred Path Workbook*. New York: HarperOne, 1991.

Curley, Arlene Rose. *Completing the Seven*. Quakertown: Philosophical Publishing Company, 2012.

Love (Aspect #44):
Keen, Sam. "Top 10 Love Quotes." Available at: http://www.1-love-quotes.com/Top_10_Love_Quotes.htm. Accessed February 19, 2013.

Sams, Jamie. *The Sacred Path Workbook*. New York: HarperOne, 1991.

ESSENCE

Awakening:
Ouspensky, P.D.. "Quotes by P.D. Ouspensky." Available at: http://www.awaken.com/2013/01/quotes-by-p-d-ouspensky/. Accessed July 9, 2017.

Decision Time:
Reagan, Ronald. "BrainyQuote." Available at: http://www.brainyquote.com/quotes/quotes/r/ronaldreag183976.html. Accessed February 19, 2013.

Sams, Jamie. *The Sacred Path Workbook*. New York: HarperOne, 1991.

Calleman, Carl Johan. "Mayan Calendar Expert Says May 24th, 2017 Is More Significant Than December 21st, 2012." Available at: http://undergroundscience.net/science/mayan-calendar-expert-says-may-24th-2017-is-more-significant-than-december-21st-2012/. Accessed May 20, 2017.

(Some of the) Daily Affirmations:
Hay, Louise L. *Heal Your Body A-Z*. Carlsbad: Hay House, Inc., 1998.

TRADEMARKS

Regenerating Humanity, The 21st-Century Alchemist, Regenerating America, Hazel, Hazel's Adventure, Hazel's Adventures, Hazel's Journey, Hazel's Journeys, building the 21st century to thrive, Awakening Inspiration, Unleashing Our Power From Within, PrincetonGreen, PrincetonGreen Community, princetongreen, pg.community, constrictive awareness, constrictive consciousness, constrictive economy, constrictive living, constrictive path, cooling tower monitoring, evaporation credit service, eXpansive awareness, eXpansive consciousness, eXpansive entrepreneur, eXpansive entrepreneurs, eXpansive entrepreneurism, eXpansive leaders, eXpansive living, eXpansive path, eXpansive perspective, reciprocating mentorship, saving clients water, energy & money. every day., simply saving energy. every day., reGeneration X & Y, Make a difference. Make Money., plug in and sell, conserve first. then generate., ferdie-the-frog, ferdie, We find you money. We save you money. We make you money., Our Promise of Performance, pg.123, Work hard. play harder., No worries. No drama. No fear. are trademarks of Princeton Green LLC. All other trademarks are property of their respective owners.

ABOUT THE AUTHORS

ANN EMERSON is the director of The Sanctuary of Sophia in Lake Mary, Florida. She is a spry, witty, and energetic 83-year-old mother of five, grandmother of 10, and great-grandmother of one. Ann holds the wisdom of the maiden, mother, and crone—the wisdom of the Divine feminine. She is a teacher of spiritual and sexual ecstasy. Experience the joy of dancing in the Light of the Goddess. Let us serve the Divine together. For more information: AnnEmerson.com

BO LOCKWOOD is a visionary author, inspirational speaker, and proud dad of two. He is a rebellious being, seeing through the veil of illusion, discovering his truth, finding his voice, and regenerating his life in a very meaningful way. His challenging journey to awakening his sleeping Soul inspires his work of regenerating humanity. Bo's credentials for acquiring spiritual wisdom include experiencing Hell on Earth. He's now reemerged, stepping fully into the Light. For more information: BoLockwood.com.

Discovering a Pathway to Our New Existence, Leading Us to 21st-Century Living

ESSENCE
**Expanding Self-Awareness,
Awakening Inspiration,
Unleashing Our Power From Within**

21stCenturyParadigm.com

REGENERATING HUMANITY
**Seeing, Trusting, and Taking
the eXpansive Path to
21st-Century Living**

RegeneratingHumanity.com

THE 21ST-CENTURY ALCHEMIST
**A Journey in Unleashing
Our Hidden Powers**

The21stCenturyAlchemist.com

FIRST BOOK ~ EXPANSION

ESSENCE is about the expansion of self-awareness, seeing ourselves through a much more eXpansive perspective, awakening our inspiration, and unleashing our power from within. Inspired action is key to regenerating ourselves and the lives we are living.

SECOND BOOK ~ VISION

REGENERATING HUMANITY is about a vision of a pathway leading us to our new 21st-century existence of human-life on Mother Earth filled with love, joy, freedom, abundance, and peace. Establishing a new vision is key to regenerating humanity. Once we agree, perspectively align, deeply feel, and energetically vibrate this new vision, then so it becomes.

THIRD BOOK ~ CREATION

THE 21ST-CENTURY ALCHEMIST is an insightful parable about a teenage girl who is dissatisfied with her life, and decides to embark on a journey across the world with her two best friends, in search of how to create a meaningful life in the 21st century. On their journey, they meet a wise elder, named Kali, who teaches them that the answers they are seeking already reside within themselves, and through unleashing their hidden powers, they are able to create the life they desire.

Princeton Green Publishing
is focused on one purpose:
building the 21st century to thrive.

It's time the mass consciousness shifts to a new story of freedom, abundance, and peace, away from the old story of fear, scarcity, and chaos.

We collaborate with authors and speakers who are lightworkers, serving their life's purpose of creating positive change in the world.

We provide authors and speakers a multitude of publishing, speaking, branding, and marketing services.

It's not enough to simply publish books, one must also know how to sell them. We focus on both, and we focus on you.

princetongreen.org
info@princetongreen.org
888.995.5630

Made in the USA
Lexington, KY
28 July 2017